Gaining
Confidence
to
Teach

*Forty-Two Confidence-Builders to
Encourage Christian Homeschoolers*

by Debbie Strayer

HAYNER PUBLIC LIBRARY DISTRICT
ALTON, ILLINOIS

Common Sense Press
™

OVERDUES 10 PER DAY. MAXIMUM FINE
COST OF BOOKS. LOST OR DAMAGED BOOKS
ADDITIONAL $5.00 SERVICE CHARGE.

Dedication

This book is dedicated to all those homeschoolers who have come to hear me speak, or stopped by my table at curriculum fairs to share their homeschooling stories and even a few loaves of homemade bread. Every handshake and hug, every tearful story has been a privilege to receive, and though I was the one up front speaking, you were really the ones encouraging me. I must take this opportunity to thank you - for your openess to the Lord, your devotion to your families and your service to others. You are indeed, a fellowship of saints of which I am grateful to be a part.

There are several people I must thank - for without their love, support and guidance I would not have had the opportunity to begin this marvelous journey:

Dr. Ruth Beechick - thank you for graciously being my mentor and my friend.

My daughter Ashley - my tender-hearted encourager, you are a joy and a treasure.

My son Nathan - my young man - someone whom I love, trust and am deeply proud of.

My husband Greg - Thank you for loving me, guiding me and having confidence in the God in me. Without your sacrificial love, these words could not have been written or spoken.

Table of Contents

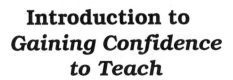

Introduction to *Gaining Confidence to Teach*

Homeschooling in the real world can be tough. Washers break, kids get sick, relatives may disapprove, finances are tight and grammar is boring. Any one of these items alone is trying, but often things don't happen one at a time. The result? You feel overwhelmed and stressed. Even harder to bear, you may feel that you are not doing a good job as a homeschooler.

What is the answer? While finances may help, and an evening out with your spouse is a treat, the solid rock on which we can stand as homeschoolers is our calling. ***Faithful is He who calls you, and He also will bring it to pass. (I Thessalonians 5:24)*** As we discover our calling as homeschoolers, and learn to walk in it, we will experience freedom from guilt and condemnation, as well as the productivity we seek.

The following chapters offer the support of a friend and the counsel of experience on the topics of relatives, support groups, test results, curriculum, building your relationship with your children, facing change and enduring trials. Remembering who we are in the Lord, and what we are actually called to do (not the way others may do things) are both the beginning and the end of our journey. As we trust God and follow His lead, we show our children the way to a lifetime of trust and obedience.

Join those who have attended the *Confidence to Teach* seminars, and have felt their strength renewed, their focus sharpened and their spirits refreshed. For ours is a journey, not a sprint. Sit back, relax and be ready to laugh, sigh or shed a tear as we ask the Lord to grant us *Confidence to Teach.*

In Him,
Debbie Strayer

A Mother's Testimonial

Dear Fellow Homeschooler,

I first heard Debbie Strayer's *Confidence To Teach* talk as I was coming out of a very discouraging time. My husband and I had been homeschooling for five years. We began homeschooling because we knew God was telling us to protect our very sensitive five year old son. He was not ready for school (public or private) in any part of his little body. I knew beyond a doubt that he was not mature enough to handle group learning situations, peer pressure, pressure to meet certain skill deadlines, etc. So we began homeschooling, one year at a time.

The first year was a good experience. Each year thereafter we felt it was God's plan for us to continue homeschooling. But after five years I became discouraged with what I felt I had not been able to teach him. There seemed to be some barriers to moving on, especially in the area of reading. I took full responsibility for what I assumed was my failure.

On top of this, as a result of pressure from well-meaning members of my support group, I allowed him to take a written standardized test. This of course, was neither encouraging nor helpful. Even though I still heard God urging me to homeschool (and I now schooled two other children), I began to doubt my abilities — especially with my son.

God, in His wisdom and impeccable timing, introduced Debbie Strayer into my life shortly after I had my son tested. Debbie exuded encouragement and offered solutions to my dilemmas. She helped me realize that each child has a unique learning time clock. I remember my excitement as I set up a seminar for my homeschooling support group at which Debbie would give her

"Confidence" talk. I knew how much it would help all who would hear it.

The concepts Debbie presented made radical changes to my thinking and understanding of why and how I homeschool. The first truth I learned was that confidence in homeschooling comes as a result of seeing why I am homeschooling — because God is calling me to do it. Next, Debbie helped me accept that I have limitations for which God's grace and abilities will compensate. I also came to see that God gave Fred and me the responsibility of raising and caring for our four children, and that our personalities, gifts and temperaments are uniquely combined so that we can do the BEST possible job of that. We now know that we must not compare ourselves with other homeschooling families.

I wish I had been given this gift of encouragement and support when I first started homeschooling. The years since I heard Debbie speak have proven her to be correct. My son, whom I finally allowed to develop at his own pace, has blossomed. The fruit has been more than I imagined.

Of course, Debbie urges that we grow through educational seminars, reading, and workshops; that we strive for excellence in our presentations of schoolwork; and that we find curriculum with methods suited to each child's needs. But ultimately she challenges us to listen intently to God's instructions for our own "crew" while confidently resting in His perfect plan for each child. Over the last five years I have drawn constantly form the principles Debbie presented, continually reminding myself that my only real goal is to hear God's approval of the job I've done.

Mrs. Fred Dunn
Homeschooling mother of four
Apopka, Florida

Chapter One

Introduction: Who Needs Confidence to Teach? We All Do!

Not too long ago, I was scheduled to speak at a homeschooling Support Group's fall kick-off meeting. Since my father lives in the area where I was speaking, I decided to take the children and combine the trip with a visit to Grandpa. My husband had work to do, so just the children and I were able to go.

It takes several hours to drive from my home to Dad's, and the trip was less than perfect. We started out just fine, but on the way, the car acted up. Not being very knowledgeable about cars, my first response was prayer. The children joined me in a vigil that lasted the remainder of the trip. We took turns praying out loud when the sputtering noises occurred, and we were all very tense. Thankfully, we made it to Grandpa's in one piece.

By then I had only a little while to get ready. So I hurriedly dressed, ate, and got back in the car to search for an address in a town with which I was unfamiliar. As rain began to fall, I thought "Some days seem tougher than others."

I remembered the words of my nine year old daughter as I was leaving for the meeting. She had told me to have fun "encouraging the homeschoolers." I thought about those words and wondered how I could truly encourage the homeschoolers I would meet with that night...

1

especially since I felt in need of encouragement myself!

As I located the meeting place, I observed the faces of the people entering the building. Some looked tired or tense. Others chattered happily. A few had looks of fear and apprehension on their faces. (The husbands who were attending looked like a combination of all of the above.) As I prepared to speak, trying to put the struggles of the day behind me, I realized that my audience was probably trying to do the same.

How could I best encourage those homeschoolers that night? By being honest with them. By telling them a little of the trials of my day. By sharing my struggles with fear, impatience and discouragement. By letting them know that though I have been a classroom teacher, and written textbooks, I still deal with the same daily challenges of life as they do... challenges involving homeschooling, finances, family, and cars that don't always run right.

As I spoke of the day to day realities of homeschooling, the audience and I shared moments of laughter, (Homeschooling can definitely be funny!) seriousness and encouragement. We ultimately got to the bottom line, which is that we homeschool because we love our children and believe it is the right thing for them. When I finished my talk that evening, the audience gave me a hearty and warm response. The struggles of the day did, in fact, seem lighter in the company of this fellowship. While my goal had been to encourage them, they had truly encouraged me.

Afterward, several ladies and men walked me out to my car. One lady pulled me aside. "Thank you for coming tonight," she began. I remembered that she had looked very tired earlier, but as she spoke now she seemed quite different. "I have been considering giving up homeschooling, and decided just this morning that I should quit. I was reading about a homeschooling mother who did more before breakfast than I do all day. She had a lot of kids and they all seemed perfect. I felt like a failure. I decided to come to this meeting one last time, and I'm so glad I did." The woman went on to say that she now knew she was supposed to continue homeschooling, and that she just had to be herself, do her best and allow God to be in charge. She thanked me again and left.

Driving home, I pondered the miraculous power of God, and felt grateful to know something of what He had done that night. The way to encourage the homeschoolers at that meeting was to point the way to a faithful, all-knowing, all-caring God who knew them as they really were and loved them just the same. They were His vessels, His tools, just as I was.

People have shared similar responses with me following many "Confidence to Teach" seminars. That's why it is with great faith and expectation that I share these pages with you. Looking at my life as a homeschooler, and the lives of those around me, I know I see and feel things that are common to us all. As we examine these events and feelings in the light of God's purposes, we can receive the strength and encouragement we need to be faithful to the call He has given us to homeschool.

> *And He has said to me, "My grace is sufficient for you, for power is perfected in weakness." Most gladly, therefore, I will rather boast about my weaknesses, that the power of Christ may dwell in me.*
> **II Corinthians 12:9**

Gaining Confidence to Teach

Confidence is defined as the ability to be bold, to have faith, and to act with assurance. Most people who begin the journey into homeschooling cannot be described as confident. And although it may seem surprising, many who have homeschooled for years quietly express the same lack of confidence. Admitting you lack confidence may be an unpopular thing to do, but it could be the first step toward gaining the confidence to teach your children at home.

A common perception is that confidence comes from ability or knowledge. As a teacher by training and work experience, I have observed the assumption that persons such as myself move effortlessly from one academic triumph to another. Though some might think this revelation should be kept secret, I have to say that those perceptions are not true. When my children look at me blankly after I have introduced, or even worse, completed activities, I often have the same sense of failure that any first timer might have. Many discoveries might be made during a carefully guided study, but often the lasting lessons and the greatest revelations are unplanned. There is much value in what I've read, seen or experienced, but the more I know, the more I see and appreciate God's ownership of my children's homeschooling experience.

Lasting confidence in home-schooling comes as a result of recognizing our limitations and seeing God's grace. Confidence that comes from my own abilities or the results I see in my children is fickle

4

— it depends upon variables beyond my control. My children's personality, abilities and even physical makeup will determine a great deal of their apparent success or failure. Methods that produce angelic results in friends' or neighbors' children may fail miserably with mine. I have encountered many people who feel they are supposed to homeschool, but have lost heart because of these kinds of experiences.

I am not advocating that we abandon schedules, order or discipline. I believe in putting in the work. But we shouldn't look at homeschooling as a recipe where you put in the perfect ingredients in just the right order and out comes a perfect product, as promised. If you have grown discouraged by weaknesses you see in yourself or in your children, or if you have been too intimidated to try something new because "that's not the way it's done," let me encourage you; the outcome has never been solely dependent upon you. If you feel called to homeschool, or in less spiritual language, if you believe it is what you are supposed to do for your child, as a Christian you have greater confidence than even superior testing results can provide:

Faithful is He who calls you, and He also will bring it to pass.
I Thessalonians 5:24

A woman I know trusted that "calling" or sense of what the Lord wanted her to do and began homeschooling when the odds seemed to be against her. Having several small children, limited finances and a child designated as having several special education problems, she responded in faith by taking her child out of public school. She sought counsel and help with the academic considerations and then put her hand to the plow. She told me of timely encouragement from the Lord and other sustaining graces. The results she described to me at the end of the year were amazing, and the very words she spoke pointed to God's faithfulness to her and her family. Success in homeschooling is not limited to certain test results, it is the restoration of a discouraged spirit, the acceptance of a limitation, or the realization of a particular gift. Homeschooling successes come in the form of renewed or strengthened love between parent and child or between brothers and sisters. Success may be as simple as the ability to obey a parental request cheerfully, but one thing is sure — it will never be the same for every homeschooling family.

My faith was built by my friend's simple testimony. God can do similar miracles for us and through us if we trust Him enough to follow His leading, and let Him be the author of the outcome.

——— ❧ ———

Once You Feel Called

Once you have made the decision to homeschool, or rather once you have yielded to the Lord's leading to homeschool, there are several helpful steps you can take.

First, decide what you believe: educationally, spiritually, even organizationally. This will become very important as you start planning your homeschool. Most new homeschoolers read books, attend curriculum fairs and talk with other homeschoolers before setting their first year's course. All of these efforts are good for gathering information, but remember, even the best idea is no good if it doesn't fit your own family's needs. Pray and consider how your family functions best before trying to fit the mold of the perfect homeschooling family. (There is no such thing, by the way.) Establish new routines gradually, allowing time for successes before attempting new and even more demanding responses from your spouse and children.

There must be some sort of cosmic signal that alerts everyone when you make the choice to homeschool. You can pretty much bet that you will hear from long-lost relatives who wonder if you can really do this. Previously unconcerned friends and extended-family members are suddenly extremely interested in your every decision. Those who do not support homeschooling may become frequent visitors or callers... to express their concern for little Suzy, of course. These things may become challenges to our determination, which is why it is important for us to have made a *commitment* to homeschool.

Don't carry the burden of self-defense alone. Allow the Lord and your spouse to help you. Time may be the only factor which will convince many of your questioners. The important things to remember are your calling and your commitment. People's reactions are never a good reason to do or not do what you feel is right.

Stories have been related to me of grandmas calling frequently to see if little Billy can read yet, or of quizzes being given by well-meaning relatives at family gatherings. (You can turn the tables and start by telling family members what you have learned, and occasionally quiz them on what they know...respectfully, of course!) Remember, other people's support and approval is appreciated, but not essential to your homeschooling. Just stick to your family's decision and commitment. You need not be overwhelmed with the desire to please others.

Continue reading and conversing with other homeschoolers to firmly establish in your mind the reasons for which you homeschool. Many of us who homeschool feel that this is part of a unique calling from God for our families. We should not be afraid to gently share that fact with others. And remember, *"greater is He who is in you, than he who is in the world."*

(I John 4:4.)

Ultimately, God's purposes will be accomplished. Our goal is to trust the Lord and follow the unique path He has laid out for us. We will be blessed beyond measure by the results.

—— ❧ ——

Identifying Your Sources of Support

Homeschooling is not an easy job. Some days it may even seem impossible. Staying true to our calling to homeschool requires commitment, sacrifice, an abundance of God's grace, and support. What do I mean by support? Well, like a good friendship, it's not always the same. One day support may mean encouragement. The next day, support may mean just a listening ear, with no advice given. Sometimes support involves assistance: with curriculum choices, a difficult child's behavior problems, or unsupportive or critical family members.

Support may mean many different things but one thing is sure, it is something we all need. It is essential if we are to continue walking in the calling that God has given us. And just as He has called us, He has also encouraged us, for God Himself is our primary source of support. When you feel overwhelmed, or insecure, or even angry, the Lord is always there, ready and willing to listen. Your feelings will not surprise Him, and it may surprise you how quickly you can obtain freedom from discouragement, by calling on God for your support.

My soul, wait in silence for God only, for my hope is from Him. He only is my rock and my salvation, my stronghold; I shall not be shaken. On God my salvation and my glory rest; the rock of my strength, my refuge is in God. Trust in Him at all times, O people; pour out your heart before Him; God is a refuge for us.

Psalm 62:5-8

Where else does one get support? Hopefully you have the support of your spouse. Husbands who see their wives as serving and blessing the family through homeschooling are like strong backbones, holding together tired muscles and limbs. It is wonderful when a husband imparts this kind of respect and appreciation for mom's efforts. A husband who assumes the kind of leadership Christ gave the church encourages, assists and protects. Jesus' leadership often came in the form of service. Encouraging moments for homeschoolers can come as a husband sees his wife's exhaustion and suggests pizza for dinner, or sets money aside for curriculum or field trips.

Many spouses have work schedules which do not allow them to participate in homeschooling as teachers of actual subject matter. In these cases, the encouragement they give to the family is often a strong support. Some husbands feel led to participate more in their children's education, and that's fine, but to set standards on husbands of what is or isn't support may be to violate the heart of the scriptural command to wives to respect their husbands. Wives should look for the service he offers the family, and recognize it as support, being careful not to be drawn into discontentment because of what someone else's husband does. Trust God to put burdens on your spouse's heart for changes that need to be made. I have witnessed some amazing changes of heart regarding husbands' (and wives') support of homeschooling or their level of involvement with it.

One definition of support is "to uphold or defend as valid." Many homeschoolers suffer from a lack of confidence in their abilities to teach their children. These homeschoolers need the kind of support that helps them see themselves as capable and competent. While I don't encourage families to homeschool unless both spouses are in agreement, many homeschooling parents obtain the most minimal encouragement. Usually it is expressed as "You can homeschool, but we'll see how the test scores come out." This can create a great weight of pressure, especially as testing time draws nigh. Often these spouses are merely expressing the responsibility they feel to see their children succeed, but such an attitude can cause what feels like an insurmountable hurdle to gain approval. The truth in these situations is usually that time will reveal the benefit of your labors. If you face this kind of pressure, remember that if God has called you to homeschool, it is up to Him to bear this burden for you. Turn to Him daily, and slip your head into His yoke, not one of your own making. Striving to be perfect or having the kids excel to prove you're doing a good job is just too much of a weight to bear. While you can't change your spouse's or family's perceptions, you can put your energy into trusting God.

A third source of support is often found in support groups. Local, state or national support groups offer many benefits, but they cannot provide the kind of support that personal relationships do. So, within your support group, look for individuals with whom you can relate. Hopefully, the local support groups provide an avenue for sharing one's joys, successes, failures and questions in an atmosphere of mutual respect. If we are all trying to walk in this calling to homeschool, we should see each other as co-laborers, and fellow-heirs, not as those who have it all together and those who don't. Support groups should not be a place for spoken or unspoken standards to be set that make people feel condemned or rejected. It is each family's responsibility before God to set standards for their own homeschool. That is not the support group's responsibility.

Several years ago, my children and I were attending an end of the year field trip for homeschoolers, when a mother of three approached me. I asked how it was going and she told me she would not be homeschooling the next year. I was surprised because she had been very enthusiastic initially, so I asked her why not. She told me, in quiet tones, that after being around her support group, she just knew that she was the only one who struggled and wasn't measuring up, and she couldn't fight her discouragement any longer. I told her that I was sorry she felt that way, and that she probably didn't know the truth about the struggles experienced by the others in her group. Knowing some of the ladies in the group, I could understand this woman's reaction. For fear of being seen as failures, it was difficult for them to be truly honest about their day-to-day lives.

This is not a new problem. After 27 years as a Christian, I can say with certainty that this is often a problem in the Body of Christ. We all know it is possible to fellowship with a church, even for many years, and not reveal deep and personal feelings or needs. I believe that God is giving us, and our children, the opportunity to experience not only the appearance of godliness (doing the things that look right in front of others) but the power of God in our lives (the ability to obey God no matter what). Homeschooling provides a daily avenue for our children to see the reality of our relationship with God. That includes our faithfulness and our failures, our acts of kindness and our moments of weakness. (We can be honest about our weaknesses.) This enables us to walk in the humility that comes from knowing who we are in our flesh and who we are becoming in Christ. By allowing your children to see this type of relationship with God, they will grow up believing in a God who can truly know them and still love them. This knowledge will prove to be a strong protection in the years to come.

How do we apply this knowledge to our choice of a support group? Look for a group where people are themselves. If there is a critical or judgmental air in the group, you may want to look elsewhere. If there is an emphasis on a life-style that you do not feel called to (e.g. large family size), seek your spouse's counsel and God's wisdom before joining the group. Look for a group with some diversity. If everyone except you goes to the same church, you may feel uncomfortable. Of course these are not rules, but points to consider.

I belong to a support group made up of families from several churches, and I fellowship with homeschoolers from my church. I also participate occasionally in some city-wide events with homeschoolers who have not all declared themselves to be Christians.

Most importantly, if you feel in your heart that you or your children are always coming up short in relation to others in your support group, try to talk to someone about this. If that doesn't seem to help, you may want to consider trying to find another group. Consult with those you trust spiritually, and don't just assume it's you that is out of line.

Remember your avenues of support. Three important ones are the Lord, your spouse and your support group. There may be many others, but the element of support is essential. Without it, we can all grow weary in doing well.

By the way, remember the lady I talked with at the field trip? I saw her recently, and she proudly showed me her new baby. She also said that she is back homeschooling. She changed support groups, and though she still has questions about how to teach this or that, she now has strength in knowing that she is doing what God has called her to do. Because of that, she can locate a group, teaching materials, and other elements that fit her needs rather than trying to make herself fit the group or the curriculum. May we all find the strength to follow the calling of God to do what's best for our children, and may we all find the support we need to remain faithful.

—— ❧ ——

Making the Most of the Time

Time is very sneaky. A great deal of it can pass without us even noticing. The passage of time is brought to my attention in a very tangible way: by my son's height. While I always knew he was growing, it didn't quite get my attention until recently. He is now taller than I am. While he takes great delight in this fact, it has set off a quiet, yet persistent, alarm in my mind.

I feel as though I am waking up to another of life's realities. What seemed like an endless number of days when we began homeschooling eight years ago, now has an ending point on the distant horizon. Of course growth and maturity have always been part of my long term goals for my children. Somehow, however, their beginnings feel like early arrivals at a dinner party. I'm happy to see them, but I'm just not ready yet.

Though these sound like the typical musings of motherhood, there is an important message here for homeschoolers. As scripture says: **"so teach us to number our days, that we may present to Thee a heart of wisdom." Psalm 90:12.** Part of that wisdom is understanding the importance of the time we have been given. While this may sound simple enough, the challenge is two-fold. What perspective should we have on time, and how do we put our time to its best use? Your answers to these questions may revolutionize your view of homeschooling.

First, how should we look at the time we spend carrying out the activities of daily life? I believe the time we have with our families should be viewed as a gift. Granted, some days the work will be hard, the stress great, and the demands high. But in the long run, the opportunity to face these challenges with family members is still an incomparable one.

For homeschoolers, the opportunity is even greater. The sheer volume of time we spend with our children enables us to know them in ways that fleeting encounters between dinner and bedtime cannot permit. We can know their hopes and dreams, their fears and failures, their joys and trials, even the small things like how they tell a joke, or what they do when they're bored. We can have a level of relationship with them that can, and hopefully will, become the foundation of a deep and lasting friendship as they become adults.

As we relate to our children on a spiritual level, we can open our own hearts, allowing them to see our relationship with God, our need for fellowship, and the truth of His word. As they mature, family members become partners in the walk of faith. We encourage one another, and help lighten each other's burdens.

It would be easy to see the days we spend with our children as merely school, with so much to be accomplished, and usually not enough time. Homeschooling is not just a means to getting an education, it is a process of learning and growing for everyone concerned. I'm happy to say that my perceptions of homeschooling and my children have changed over the years. What may have begun as a job to do (and try to do well) has become a way of relating and functioning in our home. I often find myself pleasantly amazed by the things the children say or do. I smile and say to myself, "Remember this." Even the tough times make me aware of their compassion and sensitivity.

Do I sound sentimental? Well, perhaps we all should be. Life doesn't always go the way we plan. Unexpected happenings and sometimes even tragedies can radically alter our existence in a split second. It is wise, therefore, to be grateful for the opportunity to get to know our children in ways that only the daily life of homeschooling allows. Parents whose students will graduate in a few years, may sense a special closeness. Seeing possible changes ahead certainly makes us more keenly aware of what we have today. And one thing we have today is time.

Only God knows what tomorrow will bring, and in His capable hands, we can leave our hopes , dreams and fears about the future.

The second question was "How can we put our time to its best use?" We can do this by realizing the value of the opportunities each day provides. Some days will bring deep discussion with a child about an important subject, while others may give you the chance to watch and enjoy your child's physical abilities. Small things that are shared between only the two of you become as important as large events witnessed by great crowds.

Too often our schedules, activities and homeschooling requirements dominate our thinking and push away the quiet moments we could share with our children. A few years ago, someone shared a piece of wise advice with me that I have tried to practice. This mother told me to try to make it a point each day to talk with each child about something the child likes, is interested in, or is good at. The conversation, no matter how brief, should focus on something we could both talk about positively. Though I have not done this daily, I have had many chats with my children where I learned about what they thought or liked. These conversations are free of instruction from me, (even grammar correction) and they are pleasant breaks from the rigors of ongoing parental training responsibilities. I consider them small deposits in the account of our friendship.

I have noticed that the children now do the same with me. They will begin conversations relating to things they know I like. This imitation is especially gratifying because it means they are learning to invest in relationships as well. Small as this may be, it represents an attempt to be truly interested in the needs and feelings of another person.

Having children to homeschool is a gift. Getting to know our children is a privilege. Having the time to do this is an opportunity. Let's remember to schedule time for one of the most important things we can do as homeschoolers — enjoy and appreciate our children.

> *Bless the Lord, O my soul; and all that is within me, bless His holy name.*
>
> *Bless the Lord, O my soul, and forget none of His benefits;*
>
> *Who pardons all your iniquities; who heals all your diseases;*
>
> *Who redeems your life from the pit; who crowns you with loving kindness and compassion;*
>
> *Who satisfies your years with good things, so that your youth is renewed like the eagle.*
>
> **Psalm 103:1-5**

Reflections

What does it mean to be called to homeschool? Do you believe you are called to homeschool?

Based on your leading to homeschool, have you made a commitment to homeschooling for a set time period? (Usually at least a year at a time.)

Take some time to consider your sources of support. Try to think of at least three people who support you in your decision to homeschool.

Chapter Two

Introduction: Walking in Our Call to Homeschool

Once the question of "if" you should homeschool has been answered, the next topic to tackle is "how." (True, this may feel like having to climb a mountain just to get to the starting line, but like parenthood, after the much-awaited blessed event of birth, the real work of being parents is just beginning.) There are an abundance of people and materials that can give you direction and be very helpful. The truth, however, is that you must still be guided by the Lord's direction, often operating through your own discernment and knowledge of your child.

One of the greatest mistakes homeschooling parents can make is to not fully accept and walk in the calling they have been given as homeschoolers. Many new homeschoolers, and even some veterans, fail to recognize and use the unique tools and gifts they have been given to teach their children. Out of insecurity, they "trade them in" for more common and less effective tools.

Here is what Dr. Ruth Beechick says in her book, *You Can Teach Your Child Successfully*:

You parents naturally learn how to relate to each of your children and to help them learn. Your biggest problem is that so many of you are afraid that teachers or society or somebody out there will frown on your way of teaching. You feel safer if you stick closely to a book or series of books, because that is somebody else's plan, that is in print, that must be right.

How can we avoid this relinquishing of confidence? We do this by seeing the process of learning and teaching in a new light. We must acquire some knowledge of how God wants us to teach, so that we are not duplicating the very methods we left behind in the classroom.

This chapter talks about methods of homeschooling that can enable you to follow God's lead, as well as ably understand and explain your beliefs to others. Our job is not to convert people to homeschooling. Rather, we must equip ourselves so that we are able to confidently follow God for our family, even into the seemingly unknown territory of education.

God is not a respector of persons. He intends the best for your children, as well as mine. Educational training may help me ask better questions or fill out forms more neatly, but it is not our ability to teach that brings learning to life for our children. It is God's touch that makes the difference, and that is available to all of us in the same amounts.

May we all seek the touch of God in our homeschooling. May the plans we make and the lessons we teach come not only from our minds, but from God's heart. As you make yourself available to His lead, don't be surprised if He teaches you a new thing or two about learning. Be brave enough to follow. You'll be amazed where you and your children may end up!

> *As you therefore have received Christ Jesus the Lord, so walk in Him, having been firmly rooted and now being built up in Him and established in your faith, just as you were instructed, and overflowing with gratitude. See to it that no one takes you captive through philosophy and empty deception, according to the tradition of men, according to the elementary principles of the world, rather than according to Christ.*
>
> **Colossians 2:6-8**

The Importance of Timing

The weeks of late winter and early spring are often the most productive teaching time. With the holiday season behind us, and summer still several months ahead, we have relatively few distractions. Schools have long been aware that this period can be very productive, which is why standardized testing is often scheduled just prior to spring break.

"What?" You may say, "How can they test now? They haven't finished covering the material for this grade." Standardized tests are scored in such a way as to take into account the time of year the test is taken. If you tested last April, it is reasonable to test again this April. After all, we are trying to evaluate what has been learned in a year, right? Grade levels provide information, but the best measure of educational achievement is progress. If your children are progressing at a rate in line with their abilities, they are learning.

I'm not making a case for testing early in the year. I am only suggesting that we see this time as a fertile one when we may not have to just "gut it out" with our teaching. As Ecclesiastes 3:1 says: ***There is an appointed time for everything. And there is a time for every event under heaven...***"

If some aspect of language arts is making you and your child crazy, emphasize science for awhile. If some math skill seems insurmountable, drop back and review previous skills using timed tests or games. If nothing seems to be working, get a piece of interesting literature and read it aloud, discussing the time, place and people therein.

Agricultural fruitfulness comes as a result of the combination of preparation, elements (soil, water, sun) and timing; and as the saying goes, timing often is everything. As homeschoolers, we need to have a farmer's mentality and a farmer's faith. We prepare the ground, provide the seeds, pull out the weeds, and wait. We watch the weather and keep an eye out for pests. But the one thing we can not do is make anything grow. Only God can do that.

I planted, Apollos watered, but God was causing the growth. So then neither the one who plants nor the one who waters is anything, but God who causes the growth.

I Corinthians 3:6-7.

If we can't cause the growth, we must become keen observers of timing. *When* a farmer does what he does can mean the difference between success and failure. The farmer standing in a field informing a crop that, according to its age or size (or grade level) it should be bearing fruit by now is going to be a frustrated farmer. The plants are not designed to meet the farmer's timetable, but are uniquely designed by God to have their own timetables. The wise farmer accommodates the schedule of his crops.

I believe we are to be keen observers of timing while teaching our children. When they were babies we recognized their individual development as they crawled, walked and talked. As home educators, we have the opportunity to see our children's potential come about academically and spiritually, as well as physically. We don't abandon our schedule, but we can live above our schedule. We can use our schedule as a guide, a servant; making the most of opportune moments.

Several months ago my son became very excited about writing to various baseball players and asking them to sign baseball cards he enclosed. Reading over his letters, I found several possibilities for instruction (punctuation, spelling, format). As I pointed them out to him, he eagerly made corrections, wanting to put his best foot forward. I noticed definite improvements in the later letters. There was a point when I suggested too many changes and the task became discouraging to him, so I lightened up. The letters were written correctly, but I was suggesting "improvements." The timing was right for him to obtain certain skills in letter-writing, and to stop there. My job was to see the level that was appropriate for him and not to require more than he was able to do.

We need to know what the Lord is requiring of our children, and adjust our timetables accordingly. We do not want to standardize our children. Rather, we want to become sensitive to the plans, talents and abilities that God has placed within them. We train and discipline according to our child's needs at the time, not according to a checklist or comparison to other children.

As we go through seasons in our lives, so do our children. The constant monitoring of one character trait - diligence for example - may be needed for a season. During that season, you make sure your child follows through every time you ask him or her to do something. After awhile, you notice your child becoming more faithful, so you don't need to issue those reminders anymore. I'm sure the timing of the Lord has been evident in your life as it has been evident in mine. Let us be sensitive to the Lord's timing for our children as well.

Just because we see an area of weakness doesn't mean we must pressure our child in that area. The Lord surely sees many weaknesses in His children, but He works with us in such a way that we don't become overwhelmed. If there is a skill or task your child simply cannot master, and is growing more and more frustrated with, lay it aside for awhile. The relief will be a blessing to both of you. Work on other areas for a season, being sensitive to find the right time to reintroduce the instruction.

What is the benefit of proceeding in this fashion? Peace! We all know the pressures that striving can bring. The difference between knowing when to pursue in diligence, and when to back off for a season will be the presence or absence of peace in your heart and your homeschooling. The Lord gives us a beautiful picture of what walking in His timing will produce: *"Like apples of gold in settings of silver is a word spoken in right circumstances."* **(Proverbs 25:11.)**

May the Lord grant us His wisdom and His timing as we teach, train and love our children.

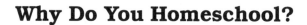

Why Do You Homeschool?

Why do you homeschool? Some days, this question can send a homeschooler over the edge. On those days, the children may have been whiny, the school work drudgery, the house chaotic and the schedule unrelenting. If pressed, you may answer "I don't know!" Family members and non-homeschooling friends seem to have a knack for asking this question on the days we feel least able to give a good answer, especially at the end of the school year. For purposes of self-protection, I encourage a humorous response on those days. Some possible answers are, "Do I homeschool? No wonder the children are always home!", "I'll do anything to get out of helping with homework.", or "I had too much free time."

Once the momentary hysteria passes, and you are able to seriously reflect on the question posed, maybe your answer will sound something like this: "I homeschool because I love my children, and feel that this is the best learning environment for them." Though most people won't quibble with the first part of your answer, they may take issue with the second. So that you can better make your case to those with the view that institutional education has to be better, let me share something based on educational training and experience: The most effective learning situation is a one-to-one student teacher ratio. (I learned that in college.)

Presenting a concept and then looking into a student's eyes provides the most immediate and accurate feedback. Testing is a substitute for this superior form of evaluation. As the students respond to you one on one, you have the greatest predictor of comprehension at your fingertips. In short, you know immediately if they understand.

Let me give you an example of this superior method of evaluation. I have administered standardized tests for many years. When giving an individual achievement test, I may ask a child how many bushes I would have if I had 3 rows, with 2 bushes in each row. Looking at the four choices, the student may give a quick confident response: the answer is 6. I can assume that the student has some knowledge of repeated addition, or multiplication. If, however, the student looks at me as if I have spoken in a foreign language, I have also gained information. If after a few seconds of counting on fingers, wiggling in the chair, looking out the window and then saying "6" with a questioning tone, I have also gained information. He or she probably has not mastered the concept.

The student described above may be able to give the correct answer on paper or in a testing situation, but my first hand experience tells me that this area needs more work. How many times has a student supposedly covered something in school, only to be unable to actually use the skill. When the human element is present and intimately acquainted with a student's work, the likelihood of this happening is greatly diminished. So I feel that homeschooling is an academically superior approach.

What about the ability to work with a group? (This is a highly touted educational catch phrase, mentioned frequently by the opponents of homeschooling.) If you have more than one person in your family, your child is developing the skills to work with a group. To borrow a show business phrase, those in your own home make up "the toughest room to work." We all marvel at how sweet our children can be at other people's houses. To be able to cooperate at home is the highest level of these skills, not the lowest level. Among the many examples for honing group skills are: making lunch; helping with family chores or projects; and making time and space for brothers and sisters. Homeschooled children also learn to become part of groups during their involvement in sports, scouts, church activities, support groups, etc.

This leads into the ever popular concern about socialization. Again, among the first problems cited by the uninformed, socialization seems to be of dire importance. Ironically, when I was a classroom teacher, it was my job to prevent socialization. The focused, well-ordered classroom was highly prized, with student exchanges being allowed only on the highest of levels: ("Hey, Bobby, how do you think the solar system was created?" "Oh, I don't know George, I just can't get comfortable with the Big Bang theory.") As any parent or teacher knows, conversations of this type are extremely rare.

The most frequent kind of socialization is not the kind we want to encourage. Studies done at the University of Florida and the University of Michigan have confirmed what we believed all along. These studies have shown that homeschooled students are better socialized than their public school or private school counterparts. Why? Because homeschooled students spend the majority of their time with positive role models (parents) instead of with their peers. Someone believing that large groups of same-age peers are good for socialization must not have spent much time on a playground with 30 five-year-olds, or on a field trip with middle schoolers. These kids do not, by nature, encourage each other toward positive socialization. This is not a negative comment about the children, it is just an observation of reality. Group socialization of this type is more a survival technique for a negative situation. The problems in public school classrooms with discipline and violence reflect this. More role models (not more peers) produce better socialized people.

What about dealing with "the real world?" Fortunately, most children do not have to make a living or live by themselves until after age 18. Prior to that, wisdom suggests that parents bear the major responsibility for decisions made by young people. This is not to usurp or overprotect, but to train and nurture, so that when called upon, these young adults will be equipped and mature enough to deal with "the real world." There are too many examples of children being left on their own with real life issues such as sexual relationships, substance abuse and violence. It is time for parents to continue the job of parenting until their children can truly be expected to cope with adult-size pressures.

There are many other answers to the question "Why do you homeschool?" Some examples are: to develop godly character; to impart religious values; or to promote the highest level of individual achievement possible. My answer would involve all these aspects, but the most common areas of challenge are those I've already mentioned. It is my hope that you can take this information and use it to share with those who come your way.

People who sincerely ask about homeschooling, are often supporting you in a matter of minutes. Once a saleslady in the mall asked my daughter where she went to school. My daughter smiled at me, to which I nodded, giving her permission to answer. She then answered that we homeschool. Fully versed by the many times I had answered these questions in front of her, she fielded her questions kindly and thoroughly. At the end of the chat, the saleslady said how wonderful she thought homeschooling was and how well it was obviously working. Her questions faded as my daughter spoke with respect and enthusiasm.

Our goal must not be to convince people to see our point, but we can purpose to give the best account possible for our decision to homeschool. We will then fulfill our obligation to *"be shrewd as serpents, and innocent as doves"* when we seem to be *"sheep in the midst of wolves."* **(Matthew 10:16.)** It is my prayer that we may give an answer that will point to both the godliness of what we do, and the wisdom of why we do it.

> *"...always being ready to make a defense to everyone who asks you to give an account for the hope that is in you, yet with gentleness and reverence;"*
> **I Peter 3:15**

Plowing the Straight Line

Fall is an exciting time educationally. Many people begin their homeschooling in the fall, whether or not they have continued through the summer. Fall typically represents promotion: starting a new grade; or maybe just buying a few new notebooks and pencils. In any event, there is a launching out - a stepping forward - that seems to be commonly recognized by family, friends, and the community.

We enjoy this time in our homeschool. Motivation is high, for the children are ready to settle back into an academic routine after the full and fun rest of summer. We usually begin some new things in the fall, so they are eager to explore the new materials. I also am busy ordering, planning, reading and preparing. We are like a ship getting underway with sails unfurled, catching the breeze and gliding ahead.

Later, as the work of homeschooling consumes us, we can become focused on day to day trials and tribulations. Being the hard-working folks we are, we tend to look only at what is immediately in front of us that day or week. We become intent on getting the plow deep into the soil so it can turn up the earth, allowing us to pluck out weeds and plant good and fruitful seed.

Let me encourage you to look up from time to time, and remind yourself of your goals. Goals may be simple or elaborate, but they are our focal point. Goals are the place toward which we aim. If you haven't set any goals, you may be moving in a direction you hadn't planned. Take time to determine a few goals for your homeschooling, educationally and spiritually. Remember to make your goals attainable, as impossible goals are discouraging at best.

When a farmer plows a row in his field, looking at his focal point or goal helps him to plow a straight line. This saves time and energy, but it also does something else. As he looks ahead he can see how far he has come. He can measure how much closer his efforts have brought him toward his goal. Assessing where you are in terms of your goals is encouraging! When you find yourself drifting, look toward your goal, and you'll get back on course. Each fall, or whenever we begin a new season of cultivating in our children's lives, let's keep in mind the goals before us, remembering why we homeschool.

> ***Brethren, I do not regard myself as having laid hold of it yet; but one thing I do: forgetting what lies behind and reaching forward to what lies ahead, I press on toward the goal for the prize of the upward call of God in Christ Jesus.***
> **Phillipians 3:13,14**

—— ~❧~ ——

Learning the Lingo

Traveling in another country can be a trying experience, especially if the residents speak a language that is foreign to you. The most innocently asked question, spoken in a language you don't know, can be intimidating and confusing. Frustration is inevitable as you seek to understand and make yourself understood. How can the stress of this dilemma be relieved? One of two choices seems logical: either leave the country or learn enough of the language to get by. If you want to remain in the country longer, it would help to become fluent in the native tongue.

What does this have to do with homeschooling? It has a great deal to do with your comfort and confidence. Since we homeschoolers have accepted the role of parent educators, maybe it's time we equipped ourselves to think and talk the language of education. You may choose to learn only a few key phrases just so you can get by. Perhaps you'd rather dig deeper and become more fluent. Whether you learn a little or a lot about the vocabulary of educators, it will help you see yourself as a legitimate resident of the educational community instead of someone sure to be pegged as a tourist.

Before we examine the educational dictionary, let's talk about another reason for doing this, besides personal edification. We are, in many ways, representatives of homeschooling. This may be a frightening thought, but like it or not, opinions of homeschooling will be formed based on people's firsthand experience with homeschoolers. Based on their interaction with you, people will develop a response to other homeschoolers, and even to the concept of homeschooling. Now, before you crumble under the weight of that thought, let me remind you that just as no school or teacher can be perfect, neither can any homeschooler. It is not your job to champion the cause of homeschooling, but merely to give the best account of what you do and why you do it. You also are not required to join a lecture circuit or debate public school teachers. You simply need to be able to respond to those you choose to answer, whether they are friends, family, neighbors or the folks at the grocery store who ask why your children aren't in school. If you choose to answer, then it is my desire that you feel competent to do so.

While personal experiences are a powerful testimony to the effectiveness of homeschooling, a few well-chosen words can go a long way to eliminating concern or criticism from others. I know, because I have seen it happen. When people hear and see your level of knowledge and confidence, it increases their trust in you and what you are doing. In other words, you can often put someone's mind at ease.

Defensiveness and outrage at being asked questions about homeschooling only heighten people's concern. Often they think that if you can't explain it to them, maybe you don't know what you're doing. If you are defensive or secretive, you will give the impression that you may be trying to hide something. This is an unsettling experience for the person who may be innocently asking about homeschooling.

When someone asks about homeschooling do we tell them everything we know and do? Of course not. We use wisdom. We measure the intent of the questioner, considering the motive behind the question. There are many times when a simple, polite, confident response from you is all that is needed. I have taught my children to look at me before answering questions about homeschooling from strangers. If I feel comfortable with the questions and questioner, then I often encourage them to answer. Their ability to share about homeschooling is evidence of the effectiveness of homeschooling itself. The children have learned some of the lingo by listening to their parents. They are just relating what they see and hear and know to be true.

Let's start with terms that describe what I consider to be educationally important. Here's your first term. Good curriculum is *developmentally appropriate*. That means that good curriculum takes into consideration the way a child learns and develops. While this may sound simple enough, it has a great impact on what we expect from children. For example, children ages 4-7 should not be expected to write extensively. Their fine motor skills often have not matured enough to make this possible. Choosing a curriculum that involves a lot of writing for this age child would not be developmentally appropriate. If young children participate in hands-on activities instead of only paper and pencil activities, the curriculum is developmentally appropriate. Looking at a child's pattern of physical and intellectual development gives us keys to finding appropriate expectations.

Concept development is another common term used by educators. As teachers, we should be concerned with concept development. In simple terms, this means that a child should develop an understanding of why a certain answer is right, not just know the right answer. Concepts are ideas or understandings gained through specific events, or occurrences. (It is also often a subheading on a standardized test.) Concepts are formed as the child understands through something he or she does, observes, discusses or reads. For example, after seeing a candle go out in a jar once the lid is put on, the child can tell you about the process that just took place. Once understood, however, this science concept is much more valuable educationally. The concept can be extended many ways, such as fire safety or the elements needed to sustain a flame. Without understanding the concept, only one fact is learned. By looking at the "why" questions, opportunities are gained to develop concepts.

A child that can compute well in math, but doesn't

know when to add or subtract in a word problem may be weak in concept development. How do we know when to add? What action takes place when we add? Answering these questions will increase computational abilities and enable a child to apply the math skills. Your curriculum (what you do in your homeschool) should focus on concept development, not just arriving at right answers.

Our goal as homeschoolers should be more than just equipping our children with factual knowledge. We should strive to develop *critical thinkers*. Let me explain this term. There are many levels of acquiring and using information. The lowest of these levels is the memorization of facts: what color is the house, where did the battle take place, who was the first president, etc.? Many curricula spend a great deal of time focusing on information at the memorization level. As the levels of thinking become more complex, we see that the higher levels involve understanding why something is the way it is and then how this knowledge can be applied to our lives.

One aspect of critical thinking is called *problem solving*. Problem solving skills are essential for translating knowledge into understanding and are readily observable by people such as evaluators. I have often evaluated children academically who score well when asked about specific factual information, but struggle with open ended questions, or when asked to explain <u>why</u> an answer is correct. This weakness does not need to exist for homeschoolers. We have ample opportunity to go beyond filling in the blanks, and we must see that as an important use of our time.

Understanding these terms should help make that next encounter with questioning relatives a little easier. When you choose to give an explanation about homeschooling you may want to use these terms to describe what you do and why. So the next time you are cornered at the Thanksgiving buffet by Great Aunt Sarah and asked, "What makes you think you can homeschool?" take a second to pray, and then respond with confidence. As you learn and use this lingo you become a native in the educational setting we call homeschooling, leaving behind the uncertainties of being a tourist.

> *A man has joy in an apt answer, and how delightful is a timely word!*
>
> **Proverbs 15:23**

—— ❧ ——

Fanning the Sparks

As teaching parents, we are faced with a huge array of educationally important items to serve our children. Many are considered essential, such as phonics and math. Many are deemed very important, such as writing and science. Our study of the Bible is the central diet. As we consider the many things our children simply must have, we tend to eliminate those that are cumbersome or difficult to schedule, getting right to the meat on our children's schooling plate.

Regrettably, what is often laid aside is what I call "fanning the sparks." You have seen those sparks. They are looks of excitement or understanding that appear on your child's face quite unexpectedly. A spark is usually followed by a rush of excited conversation from your child, almost invariably leading to more questions. How you respond may depend a great deal on what you perceive to be your job as a homeschooler.

Your attention is the gentle breath that makes the spark glow. Finding a reference book, map or other aide associated with your child's interest might fan the spark into a small flame. Sharing the revelation with the family may add life-giving fuel. And encouraging your child to do more in this area of sparked interest (and then allowing time to do it) might create an energy-producing fire.

As homeschoolers, we fear wildfires. The thought of allowing the sparks to be fanned at all can conjure up images of an out-of-control blaze ruining everything in your child's academic path. So we throw water on the sparks. "Not now, honey," is the message we send. "That's nice, dear, but let's get back to work." We fear that if we allow these little interruptions, we'll lose some of the momentum to complete all that we know is really important that day.

Why should we fan these sparks? Because they represent teachable moments. These are moments when your child's heart and mind are open receptacles, hungering after truth and understanding. It may not be the truth you planned for your child to learn at that moment, but it is a valuable and educational experience nonetheless. Can we be free to let go of our plan in order to pursue a new thought? I think we should be, and I trust the Lord to give us wisdom in this area. *"The mind of man plans his way, but the Lord directs his steps."* **(Proverbs 16:9.)**

An academic example of this occurred in my house during a unit study about the ocean. We had done a variety of activities, including watching the old black and white version of the movie "Captains Courageous." My son was fascinated with the ships called "dori schooners" and asked many questions after the movie. I, of course, considered the lesson over with the conclusion of the movie and felt a little inconvenienced by the questions. I sensed a window of opportunity, though, and resisted my urge to keep to the schedule. We got out the encyclopedia and read about dori schooners, leading us to learning about the Grand Banks. We located the Grand Banks on a map and discussed their location and features. Our discussion concluded with my son's amazement at the way God had made the Grand Banks as the perfect natural fishery.

God took this opportunity to lead us down a path which resulted in learning, and in glorifying Him for His wondrous creation. We all felt a deep sense of satisfaction when the lesson ended. How gracious of the Lord to give us this custom-designed lesson, and how glad I was that I hadn't resisted His lead.

Clearly, it's beneficial to have a plan. The order and

peace that result from planning and routine are much needed by homeschoolers. Our diligence and pursuit of God's plan for our homeschooling provide the "fireplace," a safe environment for sparks to ignite, be satisfied and naturally diminish. In this environment, we as teachers lay seasoned wood in just the right amount to nourish the sparks provided by the Lord. In a classroom setting there is rarely the time or sensitivity to fan sparks, so children often stop expressing their spontaneous thoughts. As we follow lesson plans and curriculum, we can expect sparks and make room for them in our schedule. Often, they will amazingly tie a lesson together perfectly. As parents, we are given sensitivity and discernment regarding our children, and we must trust the Lord to show us when to fan a spark and how far to follow it, whether that be 20 minutes or several days. Remember, our families have been uniquely designed as the perfect safe environment for our children to take risks and share their innermost thoughts. We need to be sensitive to the point the Lord wants to make with our children, not just the ones we have planned.

After returning from church one Sunday, my young son sat on the couch and began looking at a library book about dinosaurs. Finding a hairy ape-man with knuckles dragging, he asked what it was. I told him that's what the author thought the first man looked like. Confusion was evident on his face, so I asked him if that was what he thought the first man looked like. He said he didn't think so, but it was in the book, so it must be true. Included in our lesson plans for the previous week, we had memorized Genesis 1:27 (which tells about man being made in the image of God). I asked him what our scripture was and he recited it. We could feel the revelation dawning inside him and after looking at the picture a second more he looked up wide-eyed and said "Mommy, this picture isn't true!" The wood had been laid in the fireplace by our lessons, but the spark came from the Lord. As the wood burned, deep convictions and understanding were developed in him.

We can't be bound by our plans and unable to respond when an unexpected opportunity arrives. If we consider all such opportunities as intrusions, we might turn the Lord away without even knowing it. We want our children to know that we diligently provide opportunities for learning in their homeschool, but that the giver of true knowledge and understanding is the Lord.

—— ❧ ——

Making Room
for the Great Gift
of Creativity

The greatest act of creativity is described for us in Genesis. It is the moment when God began all that we know. To ponder this event even briefly is to be aware of the awesome nature of God and the gift He has given mankind.

According to God, we are made in His image, after His likeness. We are at the top of His created order, equipped with an understanding mind and an expressive soul. We were made to have fellowship with God and with one another. You can't observe the events of Creation without acknowledging the power of God to create. He shares this trait with mankind in the form of creativity.

Creativity has been given to us as a gift, a reflection of God's very nature. So how can we, as Christian homeschoolers, nurture this gift? The most important way, I think, is to make room for it. Make room in your schedule for reflecting, discussing, pondering, or maybe just being amazed by some new thought or understanding. Make room in your schedule for trying new things with your children, for cultivating a sense of appreciation or enjoyment for the arts. Encourage your children to express their thoughts in a variety of ways, such as through drama, art, music, or writing. Make these opportunities available, not as another subject to check off a list, but as an opportunity for the creativity within your child to find avenues of expression.

Ask the Lord to show you the gifts of creativity He has placed in your child. Ask Him to show you ways to nurture those gifts and make room for them in your homeschooling. They are not secondary, or just for when you have extra time. The creativity God has placed within our children is nothing less than essential for the next generation. Prepare your child to be used by God in ways that may be completely new and different. Your child's ability to creatively solve a problem may someday change the world. It is my hope that we will make room for the creativity that God has placed within, and that part of His image will be reflected in all of us as we homeschool.

> **And God created man in His own image, in the image of God He created him; male and female He created them.**
>
> **Genesis 1:27**

Can Godly Learning Be Fun?

Summertime. The very word brings up images of picnics and parks, fireworks and fun. This time for homeschoolers is usually one of reflection on the past year and planning and organization for the next. It can be exciting to explore new materials, as well as frustrating and confusing when you lack direction.

As you consider your choices for the next year of homeschooling, let me pose a thought. Godly learning can also be fun. Does this seem like a contradiction? "No pain, no gain." you say? To really accomplish something worthwhile, you must work long and hard for it, right? While many of these sayings may be true for adults, they are not always true for children.

God made children with specific needs. Some of those needs are different from those of an adult. The need to play, move and run, to concentrate for awhile and then rest, to learn through hearing, seeing and doing, and to be given time to ponder are all God-given child needs. To try to impose an adult-like work ethic on a child is burdensome, and can often lead to discouragement and resistance. Shouldn't they just do their work because you said so, or because it's the right thing to do? While we may hope for them to be so motivated, the truth is that we adults also know the rewards and joys of achievement and productivity. Children often do not think that far into the future. Does that make them unproductive or unmotivated? Not at all. I think it just makes them children.

God designed children to mature in stages, to be delighted and motivated by different things at different times. Very few children are truly encouraged by massive amounts of tedious, written work. Listening to a book read aloud, taking a field trip, listening to music, creating or looking at art, and playing games are all activities that can lift the spirit, as well as increase skills. While few would make an entire curriculum out of such things, substantial learning can take place during these activities.

When planning your next school year, consider putting fun into your schedule. It isn't frivolous, or heretical or even ungodly. It merely means you have taken into account the Creator's design of the children you are homeschooling.

Reflections

Do all children learn the same things at the same time?

Think of things your children have learned on a time table that has been different from yours (or the one you expected.) They could have done things earlier or later than expected. Looking back, do you feel you were too worried about the timing of these developments?

Practice answering these two questions: "Why do you homeschool?" And "What about socialization?" If you have been asked any other questions frequently, take the time to come up with good answers to those questions as well.

Try to use a new educational term in conversation with family or friends.

What does it mean to be creative? Think of at least one way to encourage your children's creativity.

Chapter Three

Introduction: The Importance of Truthfulness

Field day was a vision of bustling parents, participants, children and babies from several cities around our area. The woman walking toward me was an acquaintance, a friendly homeschooler I had met at a curriculum fair. As she came closer, with stroller and toddler in tow, I noticed her tired, harried expression. I wondered about the source of her dismay. After some greetings and chit chat, I asked how she was doing. Ann* began to cry. "I don't measure up," she said. "Everyone else's children love school and never fuss. Their houses are always clean. I'm the only one in my support group that seems to have any problems. My husband sees me upset all the time, and my baby is due in a few months. I'm just going to quit homeschooling. I can't take it anymore."

I felt Ann's discouragement keenly. I could have offered her the usual words: "Hang in there, it'll pass," or "I'm sure it will be better on Monday." What I felt her expressing, however, deserved a better, deeper answer. "I'm sorry, Ann," I began. "Somehow we veteran homeschoolers have failed to be honest with you. The truth is you are not alone at all."

Giving her a hug, and shedding a tear or two myself, we parted that day, but our encounter brought a homeschooling reality into focus for me. We must be honest with the Lord, with ourselves and with each other. It seemed

*Not her real name

clear that Ann's despair was due in part to a misconception of how life was for other homeschoolers. This was a misconception that apparently no one in her group was brave enough to dispel.

Without this foundation of truth, we cannot weather the subtle twinges of doubt or the strong gales of fear or crisis. ***"If you abide in My word, then your are truly disciples of Mine; and you shall know the truth and the truth shall make you free." (John 8:31,32.)*** As scripture says, it is indeed the truth which sets us free. Without the freedom to be truthful, we become strivers, seeking to do good and make good out of circumstances and demands too heavy for us. Without the protective shelter of truth, we can be crushed under a weight of responsibility that only God can bear.

Ann had come to the end of her ability to carry the weight. She needed the support of speaking the truth to one another, of bearing one another's burdens, and of knowing God's acceptance of her efforts.

In this section, we will look at some of the ways we as homeschoolers need to walk in truth. Sometimes we must cry out to God, and sometimes to one another. No matter what the circumstance, there is no doubt that God will respond to you in these times of need.

—— ❧ ——

Homeschooling Intensity Brings Reality to the Surface

I am sure this is a common scenario. Child A wants to play a game with Child B. Child B does not want to play a game with Child A. Weeping and wailing ensues on the part of Child A, while Child B feels that his space has been unreasonably infringed upon. Ah, the joys of homeschooling. Helping Child A learn to be aware of more than his own desires, and helping Child B learn to willingly allow others into his prized time constitute some of our most important efforts as homeschoolers and parents. Teaching our children how to respond to life in attitude and action often is addressed by what is called *character development.* (Whoever coined that term obviously knows my children, who certainly are developing into characters.)

As I ponder homeschooling life, it seems that we work very hard to provide excellent resources for our children's study of math, language arts, science and history. We will not rest until academic questions are answered and plans laid out. We talk with our friends, we read about products and we try them. We fear making mistakes that will confuse or frustrate our children, or that will cause them to not make the progress we feel very pressed to show. In short, we work very hard to help our children learn.

I must suggest that while we may not feel like experts in academia, there is one area where we can all feel more confident. That is in the area of developing our children's character. I may not always recognize a dangling participle, but I can spot selfishness in

49

a split second. The intricacies of algebra may be a challenge, but compassion (or the lack thereof) is evident in a look or a word. When it comes to dealing with attitudes, most parents should feel like Wyatt Earp with notches on their gunbelts for every accurate discernment and intervention. Let's remember, the old marshal probably dealt with a lot of two-bit crime and very few bank robberies. His job was to bring authority into the town and to stop wrongdoing often just by being there.

The other day, I was talking to a lady I had known last year when her children were in public school. She told me she had started homeschooling. She felt mixed emotions about starting out, as most of us did. One thing particularly surprised her. Her normally well-behaved children now seemed resistant at every turn. Not only was she trying to adjust to the added pressures and responsibilities of academics, but now these previously compliant children had been replaced with stubborn, whiny children.

I sympathized. When you homeschool, you can't help but see the truth, the whole truth, about your children and yourself. Had her children been replaced by aliens? No. They had been taken out of a system that keeps parents from having to come face to face with their children's weaknesses on an intense, daily basis. Now, there are no group dynamics to keep your child in line. No charts with the stars of thirty other children to compete with, or other desks to be cleaner than. Mom is no longer the lady who just fixes meals and supervises playtime, she is now also the lady with a workload to be done her way. This mother told me that so far she was coming out on top in the struggle, and that she planned to hang in there. I congratulated her and encouraged her to do just that.

While this challenge is particularly acute for those who homeschool children who have been in school, let me assure you that it is not limited to the child with school experience. Please forgive me, but I've seen some pretty bad attitudes among children homeschooled since day one as well. On occasion, these bad attitudes have even been evidenced on my own children's faces. Should I be discouraged? Only if I think that either myself or my children must arrive at some form of perfection that can be brought about by my own doing. Natural life is one of growth, development and change; and our spiritual lives grow, develop, and change as well.

God, in His mercy, does not reveal to us all our inadequacies and failures at once. He prefers to show us areas along the way that need death on our part and regeneration on His. This process is especially vivid and effective with our children. For whatever reason, the attitudes which may have languished in us until young adulthood are being dealt with by the Lord at an earlier and more intense level in our children.

So we have a good news/bad news situation. The things which may have escaped our parents' attention, or just were not a problem for us, are very real and demanding in regard to our children. When I was a child, I wanted certain dolls or toys, but the level of bombardment that my children face regarding big, fancy and expensive toys and clothes is much more intense today. We can't put off teaching our children how to handle temptation or selfishness.

Should you institute any additional programs to root out these problems? My guess is that you shouldn't, for the Lord will do that for you. He is faithful to confront us because He loves us too much to leave us as we are. Be there to love, discipline and support your children as they are confronted by you, their natures and the trials that arise out of life. But please don't feel like your children are the only ones with rough edges. We all fall short of the glory of God and are in desperate need of His mercy and each other's mercy.

I often tell mothers who are struggling with attitudes or behavior problems in their children that I want my children to misbehave in my presence so that God can work in their lives through me. If we teach our children to maintain an outward appearance of good behavior at all costs, they may tend to misbehave behind their parents' backs. The opportunity for God's loving discipline is then replaced by preferring the approval of other people. I would rather have my children's hearts changed than to just be thought of as a perfect homeschooling mom. Do we abandon teaching our children self-control in certain situations? Of course not, but we allow our children to be themselves so that God can do a real work of change in their hearts. This is far superior to a superficial act of temporary compliance.

Don't be alarmed when your children demonstrate inappropriate attitudes. Take that as an opportunity from the Lord to love your child in a very tangible way. Homeschooling should not be about the appearance of having smart, good children. Rather, it is a way to be more real than ever with our children, ourselves, our world and God.

I did say it was a good news/bad news situation, didn't I? The good news is when you observe an act of service from Child A to Child B. Or when you see the love and acceptance of Child B expressed toward Child A. These are the beginnings of a sensitivity to others and to God that results in this Scripture applying to our children:

> **Then the righteous will answer him, saying 'Lord, when did we see You hungry, and feed You, or thirsty and give You drink? And when did we see You a stranger, and invite You in, or naked, and clothe You? And when did we see you sick, or in prison, and come to you?' And the King will answer and say to them, 'Truly I say to you, to the extent that you did it to one of these brothers of Mine, even the least of them, you did it to me.'**
> **Matthew 25:37-40**

—— ⚘ ——

Pursuing Peace
in Our Daily Lives

The toddler spills his milk, the ten-year-old hasn't seen his math book in days and the washing machine refuses to work. Sound familiar? Normal life is crowding in on your already busy schedule as a homeschooler. You glance at the clock during a quick pass through the kitchen and realize it's 10 A.M. and you're still in your robe. A sense of shame settles in on you as the faces of your fellow homeschoolers pass through your mind. Surely they've been hard at work for hours. Is there any end to the frustration you feel? Are you really the only homeschooler in America who does not have a smoothly run home and schedule?

Condemnation is no respecter of persons. From new homeschoolers to seasoned veterans, we can all fall prey to the sense of failure so common to caring, diligent homeschoolers. It can seem that the most well-intentioned plans are under attack from the very start. The zeal and commitment that you experienced during summer planning seems a faint memory in the face of demanding children, uncooperative appliances and general fatigue. What weapon could we possibly use in response to so convincing a foe? After all, everything we feel agrees with the accuser. We aren't what we want to be. We aren't what we should be. Is there any way to keep going? Perhaps a Psalm written by David can relate to your situation. Here are his words:

Hear my cry, O God; Give heed to my prayer.
From the end of the earth I call to Thee, when
my heart is faint; Lead me to the rock
that is higher than I.
For Thou hast been a refuge for me, a
tower of strength against the enemy.
Let me dwell in Thy tent forever; Let me
take refuge in the shelter of Thy wings.
Psalm 61:1-4

Feeling overwhelmed by circumstances, great and small, is nothing new. Neither is feeling alone. As we see by David's words, these feelings are not uncommon, even for people who walk with God. David's remedy is to cry out to God and to take refuge in Him. While that sounds simple enough, let's talk about how that works in our daily lives.

Crying out to God is a time of conversation and communion with your Father. It is prayer, yet it should not be only during a specified "prayer time." Our prayers are to be ongoing, *without ceasing* as Thessalonians 5:17 describes it. While we may have a designated time of prayer and Bible reading, the nature of our personal relationship to God is daily, hourly and minute by minute. He expects - even asks - us to cast every burden upon Him, because He cares for us.

If I know anything about burdens, I know that they don't just come upon me during my morning prayers. Burdens present themselves all through the day, in varying degrees of intensity and concern, and with various responses from me. The best response I can have to a burden, trial, demand or irritation is prayer. I must immediately - on the spot - cry out to God with what I am feeling. Obviously, life's demands may prevent that from being a lengthy, public process. It is often just a quick relaying of my heart to God, the way your children come to you with the large and small concerns, sure that you will care and be willing to supply what is needed. That childlike quality is what the Father desires in us. Too often, we decide that something may not be worth God's attention, so we don't bring our needs or troubles to Him. We bring the needs that seem spiritual and leave behind the things that trouble us and weigh us down.

> *Trust in Him at all times, O people;*
> *Pour out your heart before Him;*
> *God is a refuge for us.*
> **Psalm 62:8**

Be encouraged to bring your needs to God in ongoing, conversational prayer. This can take place amidst the demands of a busy homeschooling life. You can pray while you do dishes, drive a car, care for a baby or wait for a child's soccer practice to finish.

Too often we feel inadequate and condemned because we don't have quiet times as we desire. While quiet times are beneficial and needed, there are some seasons in life when they may seem impossible. Rather than feeling separated from God, increase your effort to commune with Him throughout the day. Seek His face, not a standard to live up to. God is waiting to hear your voice. He desires to be with you and He sees your heart. He knows your strengths and weaknesses, successes and failures, yet His love for you does not fail. Let David's words be a reminder to you, that in the midst of the everyday trials of life, God is for you.

> *Thou hast taken account of my wanderings;*
> *Put my tears in Thy bottle; Are they not in*
> *Thy book?*
> *Then my enemies will turn back in the day*
> *when I call; This I know, that God is for me.*
> **Psalm 56:8-9**

——— ❦ ———

When the Faithful
Feel Forgotten

Many times, as Christians, we hear accounts of glorious events. Sinners set free from great distress and brought to salvation, believers restored from severe illness or injury, or catastrophe avoided in the nick of time. We marvel at these events and rightly offer praise to God for His intervening mercy. The testimonies of these people stir us, and cause us to reflect upon our own Christian milestones.

Reflecting on our experiences, we at times feel that our lives pale in comparison to those with miraculous events to recount. I've often heard it said by people raised in Christian families that their story is not very exciting, that they seem to have always known the Lord, and being a Christian has just been their way of life. These people can seem apologetic, thinking that their life story may not be fertile material for stage, screen or song. Have those who fall into this category missed a life of adventure? Is our importance to God measured in terms of the frequency and proportion of the rescuing we need?

Most Christians believe that our goal is to lead a life that is acceptable to God for its devotion and obedience, for its pursuit of godliness and fruitfulness. We agree with the Scripture that admonishes us to be at peace with all men, whenever possible, and to lead a quiet life. Homeschooling falls into the category of sowing seeds of faithful instruction, nurturing our children, and looking to the harvest of character and conviction to be reaped in their lives. All these goals are good and Godly pursuits, but our very desire may bring about the possibility of misunderstanding. In the absence of instances of great distress and greater deliverance by the Lord, can come a sense of being forgotten.

We are all familiar with the story of the prodigal son (Luke 15:11-32). This is a beautiful picture of God's great forgiveness and restoration. It is also a reminder to the faithful of their place in God's heart. Consider the prodigal's older brother. When the prodigal son left, the older brother stayed. While the prodigal son played, the older brother worked. While the prodigal son was foolish and frivolous, the older son was devoted and obedient. While the prodigal son repented and rejoiced with his father, the older son became angry. He couldn't attend the party for his brother because he felt neglected. Never once had his father thrown such a celebration for him, in spite of his faithfulness. He was angry because he felt forgotten.

I can understand the older son's feelings. Doing the right thing often has no tangible reward. As the saying goes, good news seldom makes the headlines like trouble does. Our emotions cry out for recognition and appreciation, or even just an acknowledgment that someone understands what we do. I believe these feelings are a normal part of our human makeup, and that this parable is a confirmation that even the most devoted people can feel unappreciated. The walk of faithfulness can seem dull and demanding, with mostly flat plains and few peaks and valleys. But it is in steady persistence that we express our love for God and for our families.

What can the Christian do who feels forgotten by God, or by others? Many of us would blame ourselves for feeling angry or neglected, or blame the people we feel have neglected us. While this is a common response, I suggest we consider the following responses to our feelings:

Seek God's perspective on ourselves and our efforts.

When our emotions are stirred, we sometimes give

greater credence to them than to the truth. Read Scripture that describes you as a believer and allow the Word of God to become the anchor of your soul.

Communicate.

The prodigal son's older brother told his father why he was upset. When his father asked what was wrong, he didn't keep quiet and fume on the inside, or cover his feelings with false expressions of joy. He was honest with the person he loved. Of course this should be done in a respectful and controlled manner. Through honesty and the confessing of a need, the humility and trust of such sharing can lead to true heart to heart meetings. By confessing your need for another's encouragement and appreciation, you also express the importance of that person in your life. This person could be your husband, your child, your pastor, family members, or a close friend.

Homeschoolers often feel unsupported by their pastors, yet pastors may not understand the needs of homeschooling families. If you find yourself feeling misunderstood ("You can ask Sally Homeschooler to help with church projects; she just stays at home all day!"), you may want to share your need for his or her support to walk in your calling. Enlisted as an ally, the door may be opened for greater understanding and support. This cannot be done with just anyone, so use your discernment to decide with whom you can share your heart.

Take a stand against potential bitterness.

Once you have reminded yourself of whom you are in God's sight and have talked about your feelings with the people you love, the next step is really a choice. You can go forward and rejoice with those who experience great redemption and forgiveness, considering God's mercy and wisdom to be perfectly worked out in each life, including yours. Ask God to open your eyes to see the many ways He shows His love daily, and respond to each revelation with gratitude. In gratitude it is hard for the enemy to gain a foothold in your thoughts and feelings.

Scripture doesn't say whether or not the older son joined the party. I hope that he did. I also hope that all of us will "join the party" when confronted by these potentially harmful feelings. While the cliff hanging rescue is flamboyant and the rescuer a hero, the faithful father who diligently provides for his family, day in and day out, is no less a hero. The homeschooling mother, fully aware of her faults and shortcomings, yet committed to the calling of serving her family, ranks as highly in the sight of the Lord as the more visible missionary, pastor or teacher. Let us go forward knowing that we, too, have a special place in the Father's heart.

And he said to him, 'My child, you have always been with me, and all that is mine is yours. But we had to be merry and rejoice, for this brother of yours was dead and has begun to live, and was lost and has been found.'

Luke 15:31-32

May we always be ready to rejoice with the lost who have been found, knowing that without God's love and mercy toward us, we would be lost as well. To those who have felt forgotten, let me say "Thank you." Thank you for your service and devotion, your long-suffering and your patience. Like the prodigal son's brother, truly all that the Father has is yours.

———— ～❧～ ————

Being Carried By Grace

Homeschoolers are diligent people. We are hardworking and sometimes very hard on ourselves. We often fear that the things we don't know (or don't do) are the very things that would make life perfect for our families. The never ending gaps between standards and performance seem to accuse us of not measuring up.

Other homeschoolers compound this problem. In support groups, conventions, magazines and books, the standards for excellent homeschooling seem to be raised ever higher. If you homeschool your children through junior high, homeschooling through high school is better. If you homeschool through high school, homeschooling through college is better. If you homeschool for the traditional school year, homeschooling year round is better. If your husband looks at the children's school work, having him do devotions would be better. If your husband does devotions with your children, having him teach several subjects would be better. If he teaches several subjects, having him fully in charge of the schooling would be better. If you have two children, four would be better. If you have four children... well, you get the idea.

None of these things are wrong, as long as they are done as an obedient response to God's leading. Many are very good things which we want to do. The problem comes in when you consider why you do what you do. If you are succumbing to adult peer pressure, rather than listening to God and following Him, all your efforts will not achieve your desired results.

Scripture is clear that Jesus was not impressed by the Pharisees' love of the rules.

Instead, He frequently challenged their religiously correct behavior on the basis of what was in their hearts. Keeping the rules became an end to itself, not a grateful and loving response to a merciful God. As homeschoolers, we strive for excellence. As Christians, we desire God's blessing and favor. As parents, we seek to teach and train our children, so that they, too, will meet and walk with our Savior. Examine each standard or goal you accept for your family, considering whether or not it is God who is applying it to you. Seek His peace, rather than the approval of others. Wives, accept your husband's counsel and involvement, even if others may suggest he do more, or something different. Lastly, and most importantly, allow God to determine the path your homeschooling life will take, rather than taking control and deciding yourself that you can or can't, should or shouldn't do something. The demands of homeschooling are great, and we are all in need of His greater strength and wisdom to make it.

Don't labor up a rock strewn hill with more weight than you can bear on your back. Allow yourself to be carried by the only One who can truly direct you and bear your burdens. He can walk beside you, or He can carry you down the path of His choosing. Respond to His invitation because homeschooling in your own strength isn't hard, it's impossible.

Reflections

Think about your perceptions about homeschooling before you started to homeschool. Have any of them changed significantly since you began actually doing it? What about your spouse's perceptions? Your family's?

When you are with someone all the time, you obviously see more faults and weaknesses than when you are only together occasionally. Consider a recent area of conflict or discipline with your children. How is God showing His love for you or your child by allowing this problem to come to the surface?

Take notice of your ongoing prayer conversations with God. Ponder the easiest way to incorporate reading some Scripture into your day.

Check your standards to make sure you are using God's standards, not your own or other people's. Here are some areas to consider:
Your child's achievement.
Your level of service outside the home.
The level of housework/domestic endeavors you are trying to do.

Chapter Four

Introduction: Weathering the Seasons of Life — What to do about Change

Homeschoolers are a resourceful lot. They make every resource and ability they have go farther than anyone could expect. In truth, they often have very high expectations of themselves, their children and even other homeschoolers. What's wrong with that, you say? Nothing, except when our plans and expectations are thwarted.

When changes have to be made, we often struggle immensely. To us, things not working out seem to signal a failure on our part. There is something we should have known, seen or read about. Surely a more experienced eye would have caught the problem, we think. Certainly the more veteran homeschooler would have chosen a better curriculum or made a more appropriate schedule. We often take the blame upon ourselves, when the truth of the matter is that the voice we miss is the one telling us to relax and trust the Lord.

Change is an integral part of the Christian life. Like it or not, our job is to be clay in the Potter's hands. This is true not once or twice in our lives, but frequently, even daily. The Lord seeks to make changes in your children, academically, spiritually and emotionally. While this may seem obvious, the not so obvious truth is that He seeks to change us as well.

This change, this pliability, requires an understanding of what change is, and how we are to respond to it. If you've ever seen a homeschooler at a curriculum fair clutching a shopping list with white knuckles, you know that once we make a decision, we do not like to make changes. We think that if we change we must be wishy-washy and undisciplined. So we cling to the security of a decision made, even if it makes everyone miserable.

Often the inability to make changes comes out of frustration and not knowing where to turn. Several years ago, I met a woman at a curriculum fair who felt in desperate need of help. Overhearing me talking with another woman about testing, she asked if I would consider testing her children. She described their situation. She had several bright, loving children who were absolutely miserable homeschooling. Her oldest son, in particular, was suffering. He wasn't doing well. She didn't know why, and her husband had no one to hold responsible except them. This woman had been crying out to God for help.

We set up a time for testing. Their only previous testing experience had been with group standardized testing, and it had not gone particularly well. Her oldest was in 6th grade at the time. Following individual testing, it seemed clear to me that she indeed did have bright, loving children; however, they were not being taught in a manner that really worked for them. They were bored and discouraged by endless mountains of workbook pages and were seriously lacking the tools they needed to learn effectively, such as discussion and hands-on activities. I made some suggestions for changes in curriculum, and off she went to give it a go.

I was hardly prepared for the next year's testing results. They made substantial gains, especially the oldest son in the dreaded area of math. The mother shed tears of joy upon seeing the results, and the liberty she was experiencing from stress was almost tangible. It is safe to say that this experience was a tremendous encouragement to this homeschooling family.

Change is sometimes very hard and sometimes scary. But to resist change when the Lord calls upon you to change is even scarier.

Jesus was neither wishy-washy nor undisciplined, yet He was obedient to the Father's lead. He was sensitive to the Father's timing about His own schedule, or that of His disciples. He did not have a problem making changes because He did not see His accomplishments as a measure of His worth. Rather, the accomplishment was in seeing the Father's plans come to pass.

With our eyes fixed on God and His purposes, we as homeschoolers can not only handle change, we can say, "have your way, Lord." It is in this place of yieldedness that we find the rest that restores, the peace that protects and the strength that sees us through. These next reflections will help you see change in a new light, and encourage you to become clay in the hands of the Potter every day.

> **But now, O Lord, Thou art our Father, we are the clay, and Thou our potter; And all of us are the work of Thy hand.**
>
> **Isaiah 64:8**

Diversity: God Ordained

It's hard to be different. It's harder still when we consider just how different we might be. As Christians, we've already accepted the title of "foreigner" to the ways of the world. As homeschoolers, we have taken a further step of differentness, often making us feel particularly qualified for the title "peculiar" people. And within homeschooling itself, we find great diversity, which can make us feel different again. Our challenge is to be apart from the world and in unity with the Body of Christ, acknowledging, and even embracing our differences.

The homeschooling movement offers a great opportunity to support one another in our pursuit of obedience to God. Attending several homeschooling functions in a variety of locales, I am always amazed by the diversity that can exist within the bonds of unity. Comparing ourselves with others usually produces discouragement, yet some of us still feel that we must imitate the family choices or teaching styles of others. Often, this comes at the expense of the precious individuality given us out of God's unique love and plan for each person. (See Psalms 139:13-16.)

Ultimately, parents are responsible to the Lord for the raising of their own children and stand accountable for the course that is charted, and the course that is followed. Already an awesome task, it can certainly be compounded by the weight of comparison to every other homeschooling family, speaker or author. The particular personalities, talents and learning styles in your family are not exactly duplicated in other families; so to compare your children to theirs is like comparing apples to oranges. There are general similarities, but the flavor will never be the same.

As we pray to make wise choices, we must also trust God's leadership. He has promised to be faithful to those He calls and to bring those things to pass that He has called us to do. (See I Thessalonians 5:24.) A family called to homeschool must be faithful to that calling, and must know that their course will never be just like the courses of other homeschooling families. This is because we all have different abilities and experiences. While other homeschoolers can "spur us on to good works," our ultimate job is not to compare ourselves to them, but to obey the Lord.

A woman, I'll call Sue*, shared with me that she had ignored her own instincts about how to best teach her child and had taken the advice of a prominent mother in her support group. After all, Sue reasoned, this mother was so much more experienced and confident, surely her way was better. The Lord was faithful to Sue, freeing her from the condemnation that ensued when the advice failed. Once again, Sue is relying on the confirming sense of peace within to guide her. She still listens to the advice of others, but not to the exclusion of the voice of the Lord whispering in her ear.

The greatest bond that can exist among Christian homeschoolers is not in being exactly like every other homeschooler in your support group or church, but to trust that you are walking with people who will be obedient to the Lord, even when it means being different from one another.

*Not her real name

Seasons Change

Homeschooling is a process that brings many joys and discoveries as well as a few trials and tribulations. Many who have homeschooled for awhile already know that just like the growth and development of a child, some ages (or grades) may seem easier than others. For those who have faced many difficulties or who have recently begun homeschooling, let me offer a word of encouragement: seasons change.

The problem that seems insurmountable today may fade in importance by the end of the year. That seems to be the nature of developmental creatures. Children are in a constant process of growth and change. The same can be said of their parents' walk as Christians. We adults are in the process of being transformed, exchanging our life for Christ's life in us. Our homeschooling experience falls within this call to continual change and adjustment.

When my son was about fifteen months old, I longed for the day when a meal didn't create the need for a bath. When my daughter was five, riding a bicycle without training wheels seemed many light years away. But as seasons gradually change, so the desired skills came, often when I least expected it. This is another reminder that God is in charge of my children's abilities, which do not rest solely on the quality or quantity of my training.

We begin each school year full of anticipation of the good things to be accomplished, and the obstacles to overcome along the way. When I was a classroom teacher, many students who had been in my class visited me several years later. How astonished I was at their growth, increased maturity and abilities. It would always remind me that the picture was much bigger than I could see, and that time and development were on the side of those children.

As homeschoolers, it's often difficult to see the bigger picture because we are dealing with pressing day to day demands. When academic problems become evident, a sense of panic can set in. Since we often feel that children and parents alike are constantly being scrutinized, it's hard to have a "time will help" attitude. That, however, may be the most appropriate response.

Trying to put skills or abilities into a child experiencing failure in some area is tough. Not only are you trying to remedy the child's problem, but you might also be dealing with feelings of personal inadequacy.

The secret of being a good teacher is not in having all the right answers but in knowing how to find the right answers. If your child is experiencing great difficulty in some academic area, give yourself some time to find the right answer for your child. It may be as simple as a change in curriculum or style of teaching. Perhaps there is a need for an eye exam or hearing test. Seek out homeschoolers who are able to talk about the difficulties they've faced and ways they've resolved them. If a certified teacher or consultant that is supportive of homeschooling is available, talk to him or her about the problem. Ask the Lord to provide wisdom and direction for you and your children, and rest in His promise to give wisdom.

The solution to your child's problem may not be easy or quick, but realize that other parents go through this same search. What works for your friend's child may not work for yours, so don't automatically blame yourself or your child. If the resolutions to your child's problems are time and greater maturity or development, be content to enjoy all the wonderful experiences you can in anticipation of the expected skill.

Often, those parents whose children do not read fluently by age six tell me with discouragement that they must not be doing something right. After discussion, I often come to the conclusion that the child is just not developmentally ready. I encourage them to be patient and enjoy activities that will build readiness for reading. It is always a joy to see one of those parents a year later and hear their accounts of how skills did develop. We don't want to ignore a problem, but we do want to give time for the seasons to change.

> ***There is an appointed time for everything. And there is a time for every event under heaven.***
>
> **Ecclesiastes 3:1**

——— ⚘ ———

Confidence for Change

Change is difficult. It usually requires us to let go of something that is, if not good, at least familiar. It brings out our fear of the unknown, and it may even indicate that in some way we may have been wrong. Change is a challenge to our very natures that long for order, routine and security.

Is all change good? Scripture takes an interesting position. *...we shall all be changed, in a moment, in the twinkling of an eye.* **(I Corinthians 15:51, 52.) But we all...are being transformed...from glory to glory. (II Corinthians 3:18.)** In these cases, God is the agent of the change! When He is the initiator of change in our lives, it brings about good things. Furthermore, change brought about by God does not always occur according to our schedule. For example, not all change happens at the end of the school year. When changes do come, we can be thrown for a loop and become understandably disoriented, at least for a time.

God often takes things that appear abnormal and makes them shining testimonies of His power. He asked Daniel to walk into a den of lions; Esther to put her life on the line for her people; John the Baptist to live a most unusual lifestyle and His own Son to do miracles on the Sabbath, offending many who followed religious law zealously. What is He seeking? He seeks people who will obey Him, instead of offering sacrifices that may be impressive to others but are self-initiated. *...to obey is better than sacrifice.* **(I Samuel 15:22.)**

How does this relate to us? Your family is unique. The way you homeschool, fellowship, minister and even relax may be different from others. The way your children learn and express themselves is also unique. Do not be afraid to follow your discernment — the sense in your heart of what is right for your family. As all children do not learn the same way, neither do common solutions work for all problems. Children with learning problems, physical handicaps, or older children not yet reading all qualify as real challenges. Finances, health, or family problems are real and very difficult. Even the normal fears and demands of homeschooling life can seem overwhelming.

If the Lord is asking you to do things a little differently from fellow homeschoolers or from what you read or hear from well-known speakers, be obedient to the Lord. What you are offered in books and tapes is merely advice. What you must find from God are the answers. Will God be faithful to do that for you and your family? It seems that the ordinary people in the Bible who yielded to the Lord can share a testimony of God's faithfulness. Many of you have those same testimonies. It's important to remember those times, and to be encouraged that He will again be faithful.

My friend who put her children in school is also a dependable prayer warrior. She prays for my family and all that we are involved with. I appreciate and trust her because of the way she responds to the Lord. I know that her prayers and her encouragement will be toward my doing the Lord's will. That, to me, is the strongest support we can offer a friend.

If you are facing unscheduled change, or a struggle that is producing change, I pray that the grace and strength of the Lord will be yours. Please remember you are not alone in your struggle. I have heard from single moms (not by choice) who homeschool, and who wonder if anyone else out there is going through similar difficulties. A Christian woman I know found herself alone with her children after many years of marriage. After the shock of the revelation that her husband had left her, she found herself with three children and very little income. She had been homeschooling and many of her friends assumed she would now work full time and put the children in public school. She prayed for God's leading and felt that she was to continue to homeschool and trust God to provide. Without a firm belief that God was leading her to do this, it may have been presumptuous of her to remain a homeschooler, but God showed Himself a faithful Father to the fatherless. She continued to homeschool and saw miraculous provision and stability for her children whose world had been hit by an earthquake.

There are Christian mothers who homeschool without the benefit of Christian husbands. There are single fathers and even grandmothers who are homeschooling. Is it their plan to have these limitations in their lives? I doubt it, but God has been faithful. If you know someone who is struggling, please make a point to extend the love of the Lord to them. They've probably already received enough advice.

May great testimonies of God's faithfulness be told as we seek to walk in obedience to Him, and may Paul's prayer for the Thessalonians be ours as well:

> *Now may the Lord of peace Himself continually grant you peace in every circumstance. The Lord be with you all!*
>
> **II Thessalonians 3:16**

———— ❧ ————

One of the Lessons of Christmas

And it came about that while they were there, the days were completed for her to give birth. And she gave birth to her first-born son; and she wrapped Him in cloths, and laid Him in a manger, because there was no room for them in the inn.

Luke 2:6-7

The most important event of Christmas was the giving of God's Son, Jesus, to the world. Foretold in Scripture and fulfilled in flesh and blood, the Christmas season acknowledges God's provision for our salvation. Among the many lessons we can glean from this event is that God's idea of a perfect plan and our idea may be vastly different.

Consider Mary's position. She found herself with child while still engaged. She embraced God's plan and made it her own. She was in the latter stages of her pregnancy and was asked to make a long journey. We don't know how she felt while doing this, but we know at least that she did endure this long and difficult trip. Labor began, and her husband could find no room in which she could give birth. Yet she dealt with this circumstance as well, and our Savior was born in a stable and laid in a manger, a place where animals eat. Not too long after birth, complete strangers showed up (the shepherds) wanting to see her newborn.

Now I don't know about you, but as I think about the facts, I am overwhelmed by one quality about Mary. Her yieldedness. She had to leave the comforts of home knowing she was due to give birth soon, and journey for many miles, probably on the back of a donkey. (Think how uncomfortable a car ride can be when about to give birth.) She didn't have the privacy of a room for labor and delivery, and had to bring a baby into this world in a place that was probably filled with animals' smells. The idea of that would send most of us running for disinfectant! (Talk about a trying first delivery.)

The events of Jesus' birth were God's plan. There were reasons for things happening this way, though we may not know or understand them. Mary's job was not to make the situation perfect in her eyes, but to trust in what God had decided was perfect. Looking at this situation as a mother, most of us would say that it must have been hard to do.

The challenge of the Christmas season for us is not making the holidays perfect for our family by providing perfect decorations, perfect gifts, perfect gatherings, and perfect food. The challenge of the season is to allow God to reveal Himself to us and to our family in His way, which will be truly perfect. Try to remember that God knows about the Christmas season, and that He desires only that we yield to His plan, not that we impress Him. He wants you and your family to see His plan, His love and His gift, embodied in Jesus.

—— ❧ ——

The Spirit of the Season

A beautifully set Thanksgiving table. A gloriously decorated Christmas tree. Family and friends gathered, with children in Sunday best. These may be some of the images that we see on cards and in commercials during the holiday season. While there is nothing wrong with these scenes, I often wonder if we're not missing something in our harried pursuit of a happy holiday celebration.

Many holiday traditions are delights that are looked forward to all year. Baking things to share with others, communicating with cards to those separated by distance, the gathering of families to share meals and gifts. All of these are joyous reminders of our love for others. The careful selection and wrapping of a special present to bless another is also a tangible expression of our love.

To shape our thoughts about the holidays, we may want to think about the experiences of the Pilgrims. Thanksgiving was initially a celebration of survival. They gathered as a remnant of those who came to America, to give thanks for the assistance of their new friends. They knew that their provision and their very survival had ultimately come from the Lord. They didn't gather out of a sense of obligation, but with the desire to respond to God's mercy with gratefulness.

The scene in the stable at the birth of Jesus was indeed marked by humble surroundings. Farmers can probably best appreciate this setting, knowing firsthand the sights, sounds and odors of a barn. While scriptwriters for such an event surely would have taken a different path, God's heart toward His people again shines through. Mary and Joseph's long journey to Bethlehem had ended in frustration, with no lodging available. Finally in this stable, the promised baby is born.

Having realized in the previous months that life was probably to be filled with the unexpected, Mary and Joseph then find visitors coming to see the newborn child. In our day of instant communication that may not seem unusual, but having visitors arrive from foreign lands knowing of Jesus' birth must have produced utter amazement in them. Their willingness to follow God's direction, no matter how unusual or untraditional it seemed, gave them the opportunity to witness His miracles. Setting aside their expectations and accepting God's plan in place of their own hopes enabled them to step into blessings and challenges they had not dreamed.

Often, one of the reasons we don't experience contentment is our expectations. If you expect a Cadillac, it's hard to be happy about an old, beat up truck. On the other hand, if you're hoping for transportation when you don't have any, that truck might look pretty good. Our perspective greatly influences our response to circumstances.

Being raised with certain family rituals during the holidays (Thanksgiving at Grandma's, Christmas morning at our house), formed certain expectations for what constituted appropriate holiday celebrations. In some ways this was good, creating in me a sense of identity and security as a child. As an adult, however, I spent many years trying to recreate these same scenes within my own family. Without relatives living nearby, as it had been in my childhood, it was really an impossible task. Truthfully, I knew it was not really possible, but something inside of me felt inadequate if I didn't try.

Of course, childhood recollections grow more idealistic with each passing year, so achieving my goal became more and more impossible. Disappointment was inevitable. Even the same recipes served in the same dishes weren't as good as I had remembered. My expectations stood as unsatisfiable taskmasters, always pointing out the failings.

Release comes in unexpected ways. Several years

ago, we were unable to visit relatives, or have any visit us during the holidays. It seemed very odd, and somewhat depressing. We were forced, literally, to come up with holiday rituals all our own. The funny thing I discovered was how much more content I felt. I wasn't living up to an unattainable standard. We were covering new ground.

Since that time, we have been able to mix some of the old traditions with our new memory makers. The freedom we have felt to experience the holidays in a way that uniquely fits our family has been very enjoyable and fruitful spiritually. I am now more free to allow the Lord to make plans for us that may not include old routines. I don't believe this has to communicate rejection to family members. If God is leading us to approach a holiday differently, we must also trust Him to work out family responses to such changes.

I look at each holiday season as a chance to adapt or learn a new way to know Him and celebrate His mercy. And every holiday I seem to feel His mercy being extended to me and my family in a new way.

How can we make these changes in our family's approach to the holiday season? Tackle the next holiday season with prayer. Before you do what you've always done, ask the Lord if He would like to make any changes. Once you have a plan, carry it out with flexibility, accepting alterations to schedules and arrangements as God's refinement of your plan. Be willing to respond to the needs of others when you feel prompted by the Lord. He may have gifts to give you and your family that aren't on your schedule, so be open to change. Make the holiday season a guilt-free time, knowing that the needs you meet and the things you can't do are both under His control.

Traditions are a joy and make up a meaningful part of life. Enjoy them and the season which so celebrates tradition. As we focus on the gifts and mercy of God, shown to us most specially in Jesus, let's celebrate expectantly, looking for His life in old and new places.

Reflections

How do you feel about making changes? Is there an area of your homeschooling life where changes are needed but you are resistant or afraid? Start yielding these areas of change to the Lord.

Are there areas where you want to make changes? The process is the same as with unplanned change - yield your feelings and desires toward the Lord.

How are you different from others in your extended family? Your church? Your homeschool group? Rather than feeling fearful because you are different from others, be grateful for the unique way God has made you and your family.

Chapter Five

Introduction: Finishing the Race — Running with Endurance

Homeschooling is like a marathon race. Some of the runners look sleek and athletic, while others show up in old sweatsuits. Many start fast, bolting from the starting line with great zeal and optimism, while others plug along unceremoniously. Some look like they will never make it, staggering and stumbling over every loose rock or crack.

Being limited human creatures, we all make many judgments and assessments based on observations such as these. We think Sally is too rigid and Lucy is too laid back. We decide that the ones who always seem to struggle probably won't make it, and the ones with clean houses and high achieving kids have it all sewn up. In keeping with human nature and our inability to see what is often true or important, we will be wrong many times, and for this I am grateful.

The truth of the matter is that no points are awarded for being the best looking runner or the runner with the most potential. There is really only one goal, finishing the race. As Paul spoke so well to the Philippians, ***"forgetting what lies behind and reaching forward to what lies ahead, I press on toward the goal of the prize of the upward call of God in Christ Jesus."***

(Philippians 3:13-14.)

The finish line for each homeschooler will be determined by God. When you are called to homeschool your goal is custom designed, so watching the other runners won't help. Their race course may have detours or a different design than yours.

The way will be laid out for each of us, if we keep our eyes on God. There are many sideroads to bring us back to the main race course if we get distracted. There will be cups of cool water offered by well-wishers along the way. The path will be challenging, but never impossible. Put aside your own designs and requirements, they are like heavy overcoats which weigh you down. Accept the refreshment given you and remember, there is only one requirement. That is to cross the finish line on your custom designed course.

May we all be able to join with Paul in saying, **"I have fought the good fight, I have finished the course, I have kept the faith; in the future there is laid up for me the crown of righteousness, which the Lord, the righteous Judge, will award to me on that day; and not only to me, but also to all who have loved His appearing."**

II Timothy 4:7-8

—— ❧ ——

Encouragement for Homeschoolers Hoping to See the Harvest

The work of a farmer is slow stuff. It includes preparing the soil, planting the seed, watering, weeding and waiting. The crop can be enhanced by fertilizer and protected by pesticides, but in the long run, a much greater force determines the outcome. Too much or too little rain, winds, storms, heat or cold can all adversely affect the crop with which the farmer has so diligently toiled.

To survive, the farmer must be a man of faith and patience. He must see what he does each day as part of a much larger picture. He must know that temporary failures due to circumstances within or outside of his control should not cause him to question or abandon his position as a farmer. He is often a farmer by family heritage, so he has seen other family members weather the ups and downs of agrarian life. He has likely seen the discouragements and defeats and his family's response. He has probably seen Divine protection and, knowing his own limitations well, he is quick to recognize God's hand and be thankful for it.

My own family's heritage comes through small towns in Iowa where these words are not theories but the realities of life. My ancestors were people who trusted God because they were well acquainted with the limitations of flesh and blood. During the celebration of my grandparents' 50th wedding anniversary, held in Iowa where they were raised, we all attended church together. It wasn't anything unusual, merely a fitting acknowledgment of God's place in their lives.

The farmer must remain steadfast to see the harvest. He can be diligent for many of the steps in producing the crop, yet he will not see the product if he quits or gets discouraged. It is the day-to-day faithfulness in little things that brings about the tangible results that everyone can see.

So it is for us as homeschoolers. Faithfulness and diligence to do what God has called you to do will result in a harvest. The fruits will be attitudes, actions and achievements — fully grown and able to give strength and sustenance to others. All these beautiful results had their days as little sprouts that seemed small, insignificant and vulnerable. By God's grace, both we and our children can see these sprouts not only survive but flourish. There is a purpose for our labor. Though the enemy does not want us to be reminded of the ultimate outcome, God knows we need that to be steadfast.

> *Therefore, my beloved brethren, be steadfast, immovable, always abounding in the work of the Lord, knowing that your toil is not in vain in the Lord.*
> **I Corinthians 15:58**

In homeschooling, just as in the farmer's cultivation of his fields, much of the outcome is determined by steadfastness. What does it mean to be steadfast? It means to be firm in your beliefs, to be determined, to be faithful. How do we become steadfast? We all know people who seem to be naturally determined and strong. They seem unflappable when we seem to be flapping. Were these people born steadfast? They may have a strength in that area, but the kind of steadfastness we need to do God's will must come from God. Here is Paul's exhortation to the Thessalonians:

> *But the Lord is faithful, and He will strengthen and protect you from the evil one. And we*

have confidence in the Lord concerning you, that you are doing and will continue to do what we command. And may the Lord direct your hearts into the love of God and into the steadfastness of Christ.

II Thessalonians 3:3-5

Paul prays that the Thessalonians' hearts will be directed into the love of God and the steadfastness of Christ. This is good news! Steadfastness is something for which we can petition God. He is faithful and wants to protect us.

Is steadfastness something that comes only as a reward from God for doing well? In other words, if you've failed is there any way you can hope to be steadfast? Again, God's grace is overwhelming. With Him, failure followed by repentance is greeted with renewal. David sinned with Bathsheba and was confronted by the prophet Nathan. Here is David's request of God:

Create in me a clean heart, O God, and renew a steadfast spirit within me.

Psalms 51:10

In the same way, we can lay our failures before God and ask Him to renew a steadfast spirit within us. As we homeschool, we are confronted daily by our flesh and soul, so this is great encouragement. This will cause us to remain humble and compassionate, and as we show mercy to others, God says He will be merciful to us.

As homeschoolers, we pursue steadfastness to God's purposes for our families. We desire to be faithful. God has given us encouragement in His word, and hopefully, through His people. We need to enjoy our time as "farmers" and appreciate each season and the growth and change it brings.

We can be strengthened to weed and hoe, water and protect because we know the outcome of all our labor. We can put fear to flight because God's grace is greater than our shortcomings.

The best news of all is that God is steadfast in His love and purposes for us. Trust God to see you through the hard times, the trying times and even the dull times. Trust Him to restore you after failure, as you repent, and trust Him to do the work in your family's life for which you are called to labor.

The apostle Paul, knowing that his labor stemmed from obedience to God and that the outcome of his labor depended on God, told the Corinthians:

> *I planted, Apollos watered, but God was causing the growth. So then neither the one who plants nor the one who waters is anything, but God who causes the growth.*
> **I Corinthians 3:6-7**

May we all trust God who causes the growth!

—— ❧ ——

Not Growing Weary

And let us not lose heart in doing good, for in due time we shall reap if we do not grow weary.

Galatians 6:9

Losing heart. Growing weary. Feeling overwhelmed. Do any of these descriptions apply to you? Certainly there are days as a homeschooler when they apply to me. While there is little argument about the value of what we do when we educate our children at home, the sheer physical and emotional demand of this 24 hour-a-day commitment can often be overlooked.

Dr. Rick Medlin, a homeschooling father and researcher, writes, "The hardest aspect of homeschooling for these families was simply the time and effort it requires" (see *Survey Reveals Homeschoolers' Insights*, <u>Homeschooling Today</u>, May/June 1995). He came to this conclusion after reading the responses of 160 homeschooling parents to a questionnaire at a state convention. Most homeschoolers can readily identify with this assessment. Once you have decided to homeschool, your time and energy seem to flee. There is always a need to be met, a chore undone, and reading or planning which await your attention. When there is a lull, most of us try to figure out what productive activity we can squeeze into that slot. With so many things needing to be done so frequently, there may not seem to be a time when we sit back and say, "All done. Now I can take a break."

What is the long-term effect of this

life-style? It can be weariness, discouragement or even despair. We all know what happens to our children when they are tired: they get cranky! They whine, they don't do a great job on their tasks, and they are not particularly optimistic. What we see so clearly in our children, we often don't see in ourselves. If you have been struggling with discouragement in your homeschooling, take a look at your schedule. Are you getting enough sleep? (Is there such a thing?) Do you ever take a few minutes to rest or even nap? (Heresy, I know.) Without rest, physical stamina can go right down the drain, with emotional strength not far behind.

If we don't eat in a healthy manner or exercise in any way, our bodies will be unable to do the tasks that we desire to do. Does it sound like I'm talking about taking care of yourself? Yes, I am. To some this may sound self-centered, but actually it is just the opposite. If you take care of yourself, you are more able to take care of others. If you do not, you ultimately may end up needing care yourself. Can you do what everyone wants and expects from you and still take care of your own physical needs? Maybe you can, or maybe you need to talk with your spouse, pastor, or other veteran homeschoolers about which expectations are reasonable and which ones are unreasonable. Chances are, most of us are doing too much, trying to please too many people (at home, church, etc.). A realistic look at your life-style may help preserve that which is of greatest importance to you.

Time for the Lord is another area we often sacrifice due to the demands of our homeschooling lives. This time is essential for our perseverance and spiritual health. Only you and the Lord can determine the scheduling and extent of time you spend with Him. While getting out of bed before the children may work for some, as homeschoolers we know that everyone's schedule is unique. Seek Him for the time that is best for you. It may be after lunch, or in the evening.

I have wonderful fellowship with the Lord while driving in the car and singing along to worship tapes.

While I want to spend time in prayer and study as well, some days, being in the car and singing along reminds me that He is present in my day and I can tell Him I love Him anytime, anywhere. If God can enable us to run a homeschool with some degree of efficiency, He can help us find a time for fellowship with Him. Try to find the Lord's plan for your fellowship with Him, rather than just adopting someone else's plan or trying to do what you did before homeschooling.

Our emotions can greatly contribute to weariness. Emotions are funny things and we can't always trust them, but we can take steps to encourage them to be healthy. Spending time with your spouse in a relaxing setting can do wonders for your outlook. While this may consist of dinner out or a movie, it can also be a walk around the block at dusk, an early morning cup of coffee on the porch or a few minutes together after the children have gone to bed. So often, when we get together as a couple we are dealing with the demands and trials of the moment. It's hard to put these things aside and just talk or relax together. Whether you solve problems, reminisce, plan for the future, or talk about the Lord, time with your spouse helps to protect you from feeling isolated.

You may need to be creative here, so seek your spouse's help in arranging time for the two of you. My husband and I recently spent an evening going out to dinner and to a Christian concert. This was rather elaborate for us, but it was a real blessing. Our children spent the time with another homeschooling family and truly enjoyed themselves as well. There never seems to be enough money or time to do these special things together, but the Lord will bless a couple's desire to enjoy their marriage. The refreshment can be encouraging for the whole family.

Another benefit to our emotional well-being can come from fellowship. We are all familiar with fellowshipping at our churches, and hopefully we are also able to fellowship with like-minded homeschoolers. Being with other homeschoolers can be a source of great comfort and encouragement.

After having the privilege of speaking at a Moms' Sleepover in Miami we recently held a Moms' Sleepover in our own support group. Approximately fifteen women got together in a home armed with a covered dish, a sleeping bag and muffins for the morning. It was orchestrated like a mini-retreat with fellowship and food, some funny games, a teaching in the evening and then all the fellowship you could stay awake for! In the morning, we ate and had a devotional. We followed this with a sweet time of praying for one another's needs.

There were tears shed about struggles, and there were tears shed for those who were struggling. There was a drawing together of hearts in the Lord that was truly precious. We all came away from that time feeling encouraged, comforted and closer to one another as sisters in the Lord. There were three mothers there with nursing babies, which were a delight to us all and not a problem for any. Our other children were with dads or grandparents. In fact, my son got to go camping with dad, which was very special for him. While this night represented a good bit of effort, it seemed abundantly worth it to the ladies who attended. The next week at support group, we shared a deeper relationship than ever before. Our group is composed of families from several different churches and denominations, but as we fellowshipped around the Lord and His calling to homeschool, we enjoyed the blessings of encouragement and grace extended to one another.

How can we avoid the weariness that can come from doing the good things of homeschooling? By attending to the areas of need in our own lives, spiritually, physically and emotionally. When we invest in ourselves in this way, we are able to give even more wholeheartedly to the calling set before us.

—— ～❧～ ——

Finding the Strength to Keep Going

Did you ever notice something in a birthday party , a spring day or an old movie that reminds you of your youth? Sometimes life can seem so demanding that there's barely time for a fleeting remembrance of simpler times. I have even noticed feeling slightly guilty on occasion, for drifting back to the days where others cared for me with a diligence and purpose that became an inseparable part of me. The love and devotion of a parent can be expressed in a warm and protective home in which to grow, develop and gain an understanding of what it means to be a son or daughter. The recollections that sweep over us without warning can be pleasant or sad, but one thing is sure: they remind us that we, too, are someone's child, as well as someone's parent.

As homeschoolers, we've chosen to devote ourselves to nurturing our families and attempting to meet their needs. Most of us begin this shortly after waking, and finish well into evening. With an hour or two to spare, we try to visit with our spouse, relax, or spend a few minutes quietly before the Lord. We try to find ways to adjust to the rigors of our schedule, such as teaching our children to help, gratefully accepting the offer of our spouse's assistance, or possibly even being able to pay for outside help with cleaning or other duties. Still, many of us are stretched to our limits.

Am I whining about the demands of the life of a homeschooling mom? Maybe just a little, but most of us would agree that in spite of the demands, it is worth it. We believe that what we do has tremendous benefits in our children's lives, as well as eternal consequences. The value of what we do is really immeasurable in our minds, so we are usually able to continue to give without fail. But what about the days or weeks when it seems virtually impossible to keep going, or to keep going with the joy or peace that we so much want to walk in before our children? Contrary to our logical response, the Lord's suggestions can make all the difference in our ability to carry out our heart's desire concerning our families.

> *Come to Me, all who are weary and heavy-laden, and I will give you rest.*
> **Matthew 11:28**

What a wonderful promise! While we might think that we need to push harder, or get organized, the Lord bids us to come to Him and rest. In this verse, we see our Father's heart. He offers the protection and peace that we desire to give our children. He offers you a shoulder to rest your head on and an arm to hold you up. You are, after all, a special son or daughter to Him, just as your children are special to you. This probably is something you know in your head, but it is something you can allow yourself to feel.

The nostalgia that comes with thinking of your childhood probably wouldn't be healthy to dwell on too much, but it does remind us that even as parents, we are still to be like children. I believe the only way we will make it as earthly parents is to remember our Heavenly Father. Our reliance on Him brings us rest and the strength to go on. If you've only been thinking like a parent, and you've been wearied by the willingly accepted demands of life, maybe it's time to think like a child, going to your Father for what you need.

Much of what a parent does is relieve a child of unnecessary mental or emotional burdens, replacing those burdens with the proper amount of responsibility. So the Lord wants to relieve us of excessive burdens and give us His yoke that is "easy," and His load which is "light" (Matthew 11:30.)

Why don't the burdens seem light and the yoke easy? Why don't we feel His rest like we desire to? Often in talking with homeschoolers, there seem to be three things that prominently rob us of His rest. They are anxiety, fear and a feeling of failure. All of these can press in on us, and it is easy to fall prey to them because the arguments they present can be convincing. For evidence, sometimes all you have to do is look around your house. A comment from a relative about how different your finances would be if you worked can usher in financial anxiety. The mere mention of standardized testing can introduce fear regarding what your child's educational progress will be.

Has our Father made a way for us, His children, to be cared for and protected from these robbers of our soul and spirit? If your child shares a need with you or asks for something, rest comes to the child when his need is met, or he believes that his problem will be taken care of. It is childlike faith, childlike trust. We can defeat the robbers in our life by trusting our Father.

> *Or what man is there among you, when his son shall ask him for a loaf, will give him a stone? Of if he shall ask for a fish, he will not give him a snake, will he? If you then, being evil, know how to give good gifts to your children, how much more shall your Father who is in heaven give what is good to those who ask Him!*
>
> **Matthew 7:9-11**

In a childlike way, let's take our needs to our Father, looking for His provision. As our needs arise day by day, moment by moment, let's make them known to God. He's waiting as a good Father to hear His children's concerns. His answers may not always be what we expect, but He always wants what is best for His children. When fear assails you about how your children will turn out, educationally or otherwise, call upon the Lord for direction, and remember His promise to be faithful. When your budget is inadequate and you feel like you should do something to provide, put your need before the Lord and remember that He provides for the birds of the air and considers you of much greater worth. When fear clutches at you regarding legal authorities, test results or other problems, turn again to the Father for His strength and protection of our minds, spirits and bodies.

Join me before Him, as we come confessing our needs, our fears and our desires. We will receive the peace of the Lord and the grace to go on, sometimes in glorious victory, sometimes in just hanging on, but always because He sustains us.

> ***Be anxious for nothing, but in everything by prayer and supplication with thanksgiving let your requests be made known to God. And the peace of God, which surpasses all comprehension, shall guard your hearts and your minds in Christ Jesus.***
>
> **Philippians 4:6-7**

—— ❧ ——

Grace for the Winter Months

Have you ever tried to start a car that has been sitting awhile? You know the machinery is there to make the car run, but the engine is cold, the fluids aren't flowing, it may even be out of gas. It still looks like a car, and has the potential to act like a car but initially it may not be able to respond the way a car should.

January often finds many children in the same position (not to mention their teachers). They look like students, they have the potential to be students, but their engines are cold. The fluids aren't flowing, and they may need refueling. The holidays provide an enjoyable rest and reward for the months of work in the fall. The excitement of seeing family and friends, the celebration of Christmas, and the special events all add up to make some of the most vivid memories of childhood. As we return to schooling, instead of cookie-baking and party-making, mom once again becomes the keeper of schedules, the lesson plan writer, the checker of chores, the enforcer of learning... you get the idea. She, or the homeschooling dad, resumes all the duties of the homeschooling parent.

Let's make sure we've got this picture straight. It's January. It's cold and rainy or snowy. There isn't a break in sight for months. Your children don't even remember what their school stuff looks like. The public school parents in your neighborhood are celebrating their children's return to school, while you are trying to remember why you decided to homeschool in the first place. You start back teaching, maybe not January 2nd, but close to it. There they sit, feeling as excited as you would feel about cleaning out the garage.

How do you, the parent educator, handle this time of transition, which is often very trying for even the most experienced teacher or homeschooler? As you consider your return to the routine of school, consider your children's feelings. As adults, we find it hard to return to work after a vacation, so the children cannot be expected to bound out of bed January 2nd, eager for math and language arts. Do what helps you when you have to return to routine. Invite your children back to school. Start school off with a new and exciting read aloud book, a science project, or a new unit study. I always try to schedule something fun and interesting for the first week of school after the holidays. Even just easing back into the schedule with a half day or two may lessen the resistance your children show to going back to work.

The first week back is a great time to write thank-you notes for Christmas gifts, decorating the notepaper and envelopes. This is an excellent academic activity, yet it involves enjoyment as well. You could make an album with the pictures from the holidays, with your children writing captions or descriptions for each photo. Let them see these activities as a way to apply the skills they are learning in school.

Putting Christmas decorations away is another practical way to combine academic skills with hands-on practice. Older children can take inventory of your decorations and check for damage. Make a list of what is stored in each box, and tape the list on the box. Organizational skills can be taught through these real life opportunities. Younger students can sort sturdy ornaments, remove pesky icicles, or pack non-breakable items. You may think everyone is tired of Christmas music, but this might be a good time to listen to those songs once more before you put them away.

Talk with your children about the things they did during the holidays that they really enjoyed and the things that may not have worked out so well. Listen to their input about what they may want to try to do next year, and tell them what was enjoyable or difficult for you as well. Write these ideas down as you talk, and tuck them in your lesson plans, toward the end of the year. Later, move these ideas to your plans for next year so they won't be forgotten. It helps me to just make a file marked with Christmas and next year's date and then I know where to find our ideas later.

While these activities may not sound very academic in terms of book work, I believe there is a big pay-off academically for this kind of approach. As I speak to homeschoolers in their support group meetings or in seminars, I jokingly refer to January as "National Homeschooling Panic Month." Many homeschoolers look at their curriculum or students in January and decide that neither is working. Panic sets in as they count the few brief months left before those end of the year tests. This causes many homeschoolers to apply a great deal of pressure to themselves and their children. How did all this come about? Often the reason is that parents feel their children aren't "learning anything," and they think "Let's face it, after Christmas is the time to get serious about school."

The sense of panic is often escalated by the fact that the children are resistant or unmotivated. You don't get the best academic results from children who are not motivated and interested in what they are doing. When you do return to schoolwork, the children's academic results may not be the greatest. Fear can set in for the teacher, and the vicious cycle develops. It's hard for the children to get back into school. Mom or Dad feels pressure to get back to work, and to work even harder than before Christmas because it feels like time is running out. Children feel pressured, leading to less motivation and more resistance. Sound familiar?

Some people might be asking at this point, "What about discipline? Why don't you just make them do what is right, no matter how it feels?" Obviously, as homeschooling parents, we do that when necessary. We don't give up on reading instruction just because Junior doesn't like it, or abandon math because it isn't fun for Sally.

But God's love and grace play a large role in our being able to accept the requirements of life. For our children, their requirements are in the form of responsibilities in our homes and the work of learning. As I think of God loving my children, I think of His love drawing them into obedience. His love may be seen in the form of encouragement, a success or a victory. Sometimes His love will be made known as family acceptance and forgiveness in spite of a failure on a child's part. God's love enables us to repent when we have been wrong, without shame or humiliation. His love motivates us, and His grace enables us to go on.

God's grace, His unmerited favor, can enable us to succeed when times are tough. It can enable your children to succeed when something is difficult for them. It enabled the apostle Paul to continue amidst adversity and pain. As he prayed for a thorn to be removed from his flesh, God's answer was, *"My grace is sufficient for you, for power is perfected in weakness."* (2 Corinthians 12:9.) It seems that Paul did a great many things right, so you might think he would not have need of unmerited favor because he could receive favor for all the good things he did, and all of his obedience to God. Apparently Paul needed God's grace just as you and I do.

Grace is made available to those who are in need. Grace is not available to the proud (James 4:6) but is given to the humble — those willing to admit their need. If you are striving to do everything right in your schooling and make your children do everything right, then the winter months may be tough for you. If you feel stressed, discouraged or inadequate from trying to make it all work, trying times may be ahead. If you will *draw near...to the throne of grace* (Hebrews 4:16), however, to *find grace to help in time of need*, you and your children may experience a release from striving and a freedom that can allow God's grace to sustain you.

How do we receive God's grace? We ask. We humble ourselves, admit our need for God's power to do what we cannot, and then we rest in the fact that He will accomplish what we, in our own strength and wisdom, can not. In our homeschooling, God's grace is evident on a daily basis. When we rely on God to give us ideas and then we follow up on them, He can be the Master Teacher. When we listen to His voice instead of our fears, our children can be taught and encouraged and motivated in such a way that they enjoy learning and come to know and recognize God's grace as well. We can extend love to a struggling teen, because God's grace will direct him to the truth about himself and about God. We can allow the young boy or girl time to learn to read proficiently, knowing that God's arm is not short, nor His hearing dull concerning your prayers for success.

Why is it important for our children to see God's grace extended to them? Because without God's grace, we can't see our Savior's face. ***For by grace you have been saved through faith; and that not of yourselves, it is the gift of God; not as a result of works, that no one should boast. (Ephesians 2:8-9.)***

The car I talked about earlier is in need of grace. It is in need of time and attention. As those things are given it will be able to run. Starting the car without them could damage the engine. The car will begin to run, and the damage may go unseen, but it may limit the car's useful life. Meet your children's individual needs to be primed, or prepared to work. Seek God for the avenues of motivation and encouragement that will draw out their particular gifts and talents. The results will be worth it.

——— ◂❦▸ ———

Finding Rest
for Your Soul

Winter can try your soul, with days inside because of bad weather, massive amounts of schoolwork looming before you and no real break in sight for months. These times can drive the most ardent homeschooler to his or her knees. While humorously imagining yourself in that position, let me point out that by listening carefully, you can hear thuds all over the country, as fellow homeschoolers drop to the carpet. Does this spell doom for our school years and families? Maybe not.

While being on your knees signifies defeat to some, let's change our focus a bit. Circumstances, stresses, disappointments, and conflicts can buckle our strength. Not only do these problems produce spiritual and mental exhaustion, but they can wear us out physically as well. The combination of these factors is certainly crumble-worthy, speaking from experience. If you are able to lift your gaze, you may reasonably ask "What do I do now?"

Jesus said, "Come to Me, all who are weary and heavy-laden, and I will give you rest. Take My yoke upon you, and learn from Me, for I am gentle and humble in heart; And you shall find rest for your souls. For My yoke is easy, and my load is light."
Matthew 11:28-30

Being on your knees is a position of yielding and humility. It is a position of prayer. It is a place to turn over the circumstances and trials that have weighed you down, emptying yourself of not only the burden, but also of the responsibility to find an answer and make it work.

As you have probably learned through the trials that brought you to your knees, your own solutions have fallen short. Your plans have not worked out. All your hard work has not made the needed change in yourself, your children, your spouse, your finances — your life. In God's mercy He has allowed you to come to the end of your means to change things. Now He would like to relieve you of the burden you are unable to carry any longer.

The image of the yoke is a good one. It guides and directs the wearer, yet it doesn't constrict or bind. It distributes the weight and pressure evenly, so that all effort is put to maximum use, creating the greatest productivity. A yoke gives the driver the ability to direct the wearers from behind, where there's a vantage point. The wearers of the yoke don't have to worry about direction, they can trust the driver's ability to see ahead and avoid pitfalls. A yoke is not painful to the wearer, unless it is too heavy or the wearer strains against it, going in an opposite direction or refusing to start or stop. In short, pain comes from resisting the yoke's direction.

Yokes in Scripture also denote partnerships, teams, and more than one working together. Here again the Giver of the yoke meets us while we are on our knees and brings us back to productivity. He is the one with the vantage point. He is the one with the perfectly sized yoke and the perfect team. The team may include your spouse, your family or your brothers and sisters in Christ, but it will always include our Lord as well. His direction is secure. The only question is our participation. Will we agree with the One giving direction? Will we trust the size and shape of the yoke He has given us?

Sometimes we try to make a yoke ourselves, hoping to substitute ours for God's. We mold it and shape it using our sense of what should be done. Then we ask the Lord to make it work. ("I can't homeschool my high schooler because it's too hard and too scary for me, so

Lord please bless my decision to put him in school." Or, "I can't change curriculums because good Christian homeschoolers always homeschool this way no matter what. We will continue to homeschool this way even though we are all miserable, so Lord please bless my decision.") In each circumstance, you may be doing what is right, and you should stand firm in the face of fear and opposition. Often though, we are not open to doing things differently from what we expect, or from what we see others doing. The rest we are seeking can't be achieved through this kind of decision making.

How can we slip our head into the yoke that will be light, with the burden that is bearable? (1) By identifying the things that brought us to our knees, (2) by giving these trials and circumstances to the Lord, and (3) by releasing the responsibility and the outcome to Him. Does that mean you stop giving direction to the contrary 13-year-old? No. It means that you do what you think is right, then step back. Ranting, raving and rebellion may result, but the Lord certainly has a plan for this young person.

We often must allow room for God and life to work on our young charges. Consequences may have to be your child's teacher for awhile. (Reasonable amounts of school work not done in reasonable amounts of time may equal homework that night.) Does this seem insensitive? It may feel uncomfortable if you are used to accepting responsibility for everything getting done. It may, however, be the first step toward peace in your life.

Talk with your spouse or a mature Christian you trust, and evaluate the causes of your stress and the scope of the problems you are trying to address. It may be that your spouse has been suggesting a solution for a long time, and you have been resisting it. It may be that the Lord has shown you something that you are afraid to implement because of the conflicts that could arise. You may have been given advice about your curriculum or schedule that you were unwilling to attempt. Wherever you have put up a roadblock, prayerfully ask the Lord to start taking it down. He will be gentle, yet if you allow

Him, He will be firm. If you let Him help you His way, you may find a place of rest you never knew existed.

In the meantime, don't get down on yourself. Don't give up doing all you know to do that is right. If you have given up, get started again with at least one thing you know you should do. Have devotions with the kids, have devotions by yourself, do some school work, fellowship, etc.   Cling to the truth of the Scripture, and remember you are not alone.

> **Since then we have a great high priest who has passed through the heavens, Jesus, the Son of God, let us hold fast our confession. For we do not have a high priest who cannot sympathize with our weaknesses, but one who has been tempted in all things as we are, yet without sin. Let us therefore draw near with confidence to the throne of grace, that we may receive mercy and may find grace to help in time of need.**
>
> **Hebrews 4:14-16**

Reflections

Write down some goals for your homeschooling. You can't be general, or specific for each child. (Remember, there are no correct answers that you need to conform to.) Write what the Lord has put in your heart.

Think of areas in which you and your children have made progress. You may want to keep an "Encouragement List" to look at on those not so great days. Remember, even small successes are encouraging.

Are there areas of your life that have become burdens? Bring these specific problems to the Lord and ask Him to carry them. You may want to write down these prayers so that you can be encouraged by His answers.

Remember that God's grace is available to those in need. It will be sufficient to meet your needs, no matter how small or great they are. Ask Him for His grace to meet your needs. Draw near to His throne of grace.

Chapter Six

Introduction: Navigating the Sometimes Rough Waters of Family & Friends

If you are blessed with supportive extended family and friends, please continue reading anyway. It is wonderful to have such support, but it is far from common. As you read this chapter, think of those homeschoolers you know or fellowship with. Look for insights into the pressures they face and ways you can be more understanding and supportive of them. You might even think about sharing those loving, supportive grandparents with some homeschooling family who may not be so fortunate. As we try to support others, we will gain a compassion that pleases God, and a greater love for those He died for.

Beginning the journey as a homeschooler is a big step which can be quite intimidating. For many homeschoolers, this step is made even harder by the reactions of family and friends. Continuing in spite of criticism, doubt or even hostility is not always easy.

We are raised from an early age to seek our parents' approval. While this is good and entirely scriptural as children, things change when we become parents. Even after the process of *leaving and cleaving* from parents to wife or husband, many of us still want to please our family, and there is nothing wrong with that. Scripture admonishes us to *honor our mother and father*, which takes the form of respect, consideration and attention. I believe, however, that it is possible to honor your parents while choosing a course of action for your family that is not the same as their choice might have been.

Many times I have listened to homeschoolers tell me how hurt they are by their families' reactions. For many, this is simply part of the cost of homeschooling. They are no longer doing what everyone else does, or what their parents did.

When we accept Christ, we understand that we are going to follow a path of God's making, not our own. Responding to God's call to homeschool involves the same kind of understanding. We will be doing things differently. That is why it is essential to know in your heart that homeschooling is what you are supposed to do. When you are sure of that fact, you have begun to find the strength and peace that will carry you through your relationship trials.

I have a friend whose sister strongly opposes her homeschooling. When I see this woman's sister around town, she tells me that Sandy* is crazy for keeping her children home. How do I respond? I smile and say, "She looked fine the last time I saw her."

As you can imagine, this in-your-face kind of criticism is no picnic for Sandy at family gatherings. Over time, she has gained a "turn the other cheek" approach to her sister, and makes a determined effort not to be lured into an argument. This is an excellent approach, especially since there is nothing she can say to change her sister's mind. From where does her strength come? It comes from knowing she is obeying God.

It's easy enough to understand why non-Christian family and friends may not support your homeschooling. After all they don't know the Lord. But what do you do when church friends are unsupportive or Christian family members express doubt? Hopefully, you will be gracious in your response, but no less firm than with the unsaved.

*Not her real name

God calls His people to function differently. He gives us different gifts, different talents, different spheres of influence. Once we have determined our calling to homeschool, we stand once again on obeying God. Other believers or even pastors are not responsible for your children. You are.

Why am I going to such lengths to remind you of His calling? Because it will make all the difference in how you respond to the feelings of others. If God has brought you down this path, then it is His job to see you through. If you can be secure in that, then the feelings of others can be weighed and evaluated without fear or defensiveness. You can actually consider the comments of that outspoken family member, glean whatever truth may be there and disregard whatever may be an attack on your obedience to God. Scripture warns us there will be times when families won't agree. Sometimes that is just hard for us to believe.

And He said to them, "Truly I say to you, there is no one who has left house or wife or brothers or parents or children, for the sake of the kingdom of God, who shall not receive many times as much at this time and in the age to come, eternal life."

Luke 18:29,30

As you continue on the path God has called you, many of your critics will fade away. Time will ease their fears, and they may become great supporters of homeschooling. Give them the opportunity to change, remembering that the mercy you extend to others is the same mercy you will receive from God.

When we first began homeschooling, my father was less than thrilled. As he has seen his grandchildren grow and the public schools become more ineffective and even dangerous, he has become a supporter of homeschooling. This is not unusual, but is actually becoming more common.

A special note to single parent homeschoolers or those with marginally supportive spouses: I encourage you to remember that God's arm is not short, nor is His hearing dull. As you bring your desires to homeschool before Him, He will answer your prayers. Trust Him, even if it means your children must remain in school for a season before you can begin. His plan is for your good and your children's, and you must never allow the enemy to tell you otherwise. God will be faithful! I do believe that married people who homeschool should receive some sort of agreement from their spouses, even if it is only, "We'll see how it goes." Homeschooling in opposition to one's spouse may create hostility and stress that is too difficult to bear.

I once had a father call me from across the state, requesting that I test his homeschooled daughter. He wanted to come on Saturday (in three days) and he stated that if she wasn't on grade level, she was going back to private school on Monday. I agreed to do the testing, and immediately began to pray. The mother called me the next day, hysterical. She was afraid she had failed to teach her daughter well, and she couldn't bear her daughter having to go back to private school. I encouraged her to trust God, and to hang on until after the testing. I felt great compassion for this woman who was so distraught.

Saturday came, and the father and daughter arrived. The girl seemed sweet and understandably stressed. We tried to relax some by talking about her favorite activities, and then we began the test. This young lady scored grade level or above in every subject. When I shared the results with the father, he gave a huge sigh of relief. He explained that he had been so worried about his daughter's progress because of his wife's extreme lack of confidence. He said that he only wanted what was best for his family.

Seeing him as a concerned father, instead of an ogre, I shared with him that the best thing he could do for his daughter was to support and encourage his wife. The peace that came over us both was confirmation that we were indeed on the right track. He left determining to do just that. The wife called me several days later to thank me and I reminded her that she was the one who had done the work. We agreed that God had indeed been faithful to them, and that He always would be.

No matter what your situation, remember that our salvation does not come from flesh and blood, but from the God who gave us these children in the first place.

Families Matter

Some days we all wish we could homeschool on a fully equipped but remote desert island. The phone rings during an incredibly wonderful (or terrible) school lesson, and you hear the voice of a relative asking how homeschooling is going. Many who have homeschooled a few years have experienced this, and know that depending on the relative, the answer could be crucial.

My personal favorite answer is, "Just fine! Wonderful actually." (As I make furious hand motions to the children not to make a SOUND while I am on the phone.)

Of course there are many wonderful family members who fully support the decision made by a couple to homeschool and can be a source of great strength and encouragement. If this is your situation, give them a pat on the back and make sure you are counting your blessings.

Many homeschoolers struggle a great deal with skepticism or even hostility demonstrated by their families. For some, these trials come on a daily basis. The insecurity many new homeschoolers feel can be compounded by a single comment from a well-meaning relative. How can we, as Christian homeschoolers, deal with these pressures without throwing up our hands? Here are some suggestions.

1. Take refuge in the Lord.

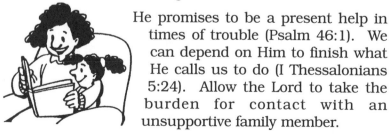

He promises to be a present help in times of trouble (Psalm 46:1). We can depend on Him to finish what He calls us to do (I Thessalonians 5:24). Allow the Lord to take the burden for contact with an unsupportive family member.

2. Allow God's order to protect you.

Most of those who encounter this criticism are women, so share this struggle with your husband. If it is the husband's family expressing reservations, this can be very hurtful to the wife, so appeal to your husband for wisdom, guidance and support in handling any response. Try to keep your husband informed of your needs in this area, as he may be unaware of the depth of the conflict for you. Join together with your husband in specific prayer about this conflict. (Matthew 18:19-20) If you are without the covering of a husband, you may want to seek the support and counsel of a trusted friend, relative or pastor.

3. Be informed.

Many of those who attack or criticize homeschooling are really uninformed. Being able to calmly answer questions that are posed to you may go a long way in fostering acceptance among family members. On the other hand, being defensive and argumentative will only increase concern. There are many resources available today which give legal and educational information about homeschooling. For the most part, relatives and friends are well-meaning. Try to give a gracious answer to those who are learning to cope with your decision.

4. Time is usually on your side.

Anything that is new may encounter resistance, so give family and friends time to see some results. As we are diligent, God seems pleased to bless our efforts. I have many times seen His faithfulness in changing hearts toward homeschoolers. My father, who is a very intelligent and successful pilot, had his concerns at first, but has become a strong supporter of our homeschooling over the years. His desire was simply for his grandchildren to do well. As he saw them excelling in our homeschool, his support and encouragement followed. Of course this means a great deal to us as a family.

The decision to homeschool is not one that should be made lightly, yet with the Lord's guidance and direction we can remain faithful to His calling even through rough circumstances like family resistance. His grace is sufficient to meet all our needs as homeschoolers.

> ***And He has said to me, "My grace is sufficient for you, for power is perfected in weakness." Most gladly, therefore, I will rather boast about my weaknesses, that the power of Christ may dwell in me.***
>
> **II Corinthians 12:9**

Avoiding Holiday Traps

The holidays are a busy time of year. Normal routines and schedules can dissolve with word of a living nativity scene nearby, or a session of caroling down the street. Relatives drop by unannounced, and things have to be done on the spur of the moment. After striving for order for months and feeling like you've finally arrived at some, it may seem to disintegrate at the ring of a phone, a knock at the door or the sight of an overtired child who stayed up for something special.

Homeschoolers often find themselves in one of two undesirable positions. They either give up doing school earlier than they planned (out of frustration), or they become drill sergeants that insist on work as normal no matter what. At some point, you must decide how your family will approach the holiday season. If you can bring yourself to envision how you will feel about outings, parties, visiting, playtime, etc., now, you can handle the consequences more effectively, and in a way that may spare your emotions, when those events actually come.

Here are some possible scenarios and their results. You decide to make decisions about extra activities on a day-to-day basis. After awhile, you realize you have been directing your children to start at the same unfinished page over and over. Feelings of unproductiveness and futility set in, followed by just throwing up your hands and plopping on the couch. If you're not careful, feelings of guilt crop up and spread to other areas of your thoughts, culminating in the big question, "Have we really accomplished anything?" If you reach this point, I suggest getting out any work your children have completed and reading it as quickly as possible. Remind yourself that it wasn't always this hectic.

What is the solution to this scenario? I have learned to adjust my expectations during the holidays. I reduce the amount of work I plan for the children to accomplish, and then I prepare myself to be flexible. This is usually not an easy thing for homeschoolers to do. While lowering my expectations for academic output, I raise my expectations in the areas of music appreciation, thinking of others outside our immediate family, and being open to the spiritual lessons that abound. In adjusting your expectations, you can more confidently stick to your guns when you have to say "No" to an activity, and you can more fully enjoy the ones to which you say "Yes."

Homeschoolers often feel insecure in their ability to incorporate art and music into their curriculum. The holiday season provides a perfect opportunity to make time for activities in art, music and drama. Possible avenues for these experiences are choir presentations, dramas and ballets, as well as orchestra performance of such classics as Handel's <u>Messiah</u>. Making small gifts brings great satisfaction to children and parents. Craft books are widely available and all contain easy-to-do projects. Record these activities in your school log, as they constitute legitimate and valuable learning activities.

Setting a date for taking a break from school often helps, too. If you plan to do school throughout the holidays, you may begin to resent every interruption, no matter what it is. Like it or not, once the public schools are out for vacation, most people won't understand why you are still doing school. Talk with your spouse about how to be realistic with your planning. Parties and field trips every day of the week would probably wipe everyone out, but exceptions can be made for the unique activities available.

Here is a second kind of scenario. You decide that no matter what, you will continue to do school, and you implement extreme measures to do so. You rise earlier to do school before a field trip, you do school at night or on Saturdays, etc. The message to your family may be, "Fun will cost you. No matter how good the activity, you still have to finish your work." You do this because you do not want your children to grow up seeing holidays and family outings as interruptions to the really important job of life: getting our work done!

Many homeschoolers adopt this attitude out of fear. They fear that they won't get enough completed and they'll be hopelessly behind by June when their child will be unprepared for end of the year tests. It may seem like a big jump from time off at Christmas to year-end failure, but remember, fear is an unreasonable thing. For some people, allowing one exception is just the beginning of an avalanche, or so they fear. "If I lose momentum at Christmas, I may never get it back," they think.

The solution for these feelings is the same as the solution to the first scenario. Sit down and think ahead. We've all done school at some time when we should have taken a break. The frustration and difficulties that resulted should have helped us see that we can't set standards for perfect homeschooling and then kill ourselves to meet them. Over and above the emotional negatives, I truly question the permanence of things learned under duress. We all acknowledge the damage done in public school when inappropriate pressure is put on children to work. Let's examine our own practices for pressure we put on ourselves and our children as a result of our fears.

As you consider your holiday schedule, try to think openly about an activity before you automatically resist it. Allow the Lord to guide your selection of special events, and don't just reject everything as being trivial or unproductive. Keep a calendar with you so you can feel like you are maintaining a sense of control over your schedule. Try not to give people the feeling that their events are just interruptions to your much more important schoolwork. Jesus addressed the valuing of things or actions over people. He spoke to the Pharisees often about the emptiness of their rituals, and their choosing appearances over true sacrifice and love.

Jesus is the best example of someone who adjusted a schedule and was totally flexible and open. When visiting in the home of Mary and Martha, Jesus gently reminded

Martha that doing even good things, cannot compare to fellowshipping with the Lord. He may want you to fellowship at a time when you're thinking only of work. Be open to being drawn to sit at His feet, along with your children. Fellowship may come at a time when it is not scheduled, or in a place you don't expect it. Having eyes to see these opportunities and the heart to respond was the attitude of Mary as she sat at the Lord's feet.

If we seek the Lord during the holidays, I believe we can have greater success in avoiding the traps of guilt and fear in regard to our schooling. He has a plan for your family's holiday season, and He desires the fullness of the season for each one of us. As you consider activities, ask yourself why you are saying "Yes" or "No." Pray for guidance and then trust God to be able to give you the wisdom to make decisions.

I pray that you will experience the peace of the Lord during the holiday season. His peace refreshes and restores, so that when we go back to the work of school we will do so with renewed strength and resolve. Let us recognize and celebrate the coming of our King into these areas of our lives. Happy Holidays.

> *Now as they were traveling along, He entered a certain village; and a woman named Martha welcomed Him into her home. And she had a sister called Mary, who moreover was listening to the Lord's word, seated at His feet. But Martha was distracted with all her preparations; and she came up to Him, and said, "Lord, do You care not that my sister has left me to do all the serving alone? Then tell her to help me." But the Lord answered and said to her, "Martha, Martha, you are so worried and bothered about so many things; but only a few things are necessary, really only one, for Mary has chosen the good part, which shall not be taken away from her."*
>
> **Luke 10:38-42**

——— ❧ ———

Park Day Possibilities

Park Day. Support group meetings. The one day a month when homeschoolers arise, pack lunches, pack cars and pack parks. These days are generally looked forward to as times of fun and fellowship, as well as time for participating in group activities such as book reports, science projects and presentations. Moms (and dads and sometimes grandparents) come to these days to enjoy the company of other homeschoolers and their families. While it may seem to be a hectic, harried sort of day for most, it can be a day to gather information, receive encouragement and gain a little perspective on your daily life as a homeschooler.

Park Day holds many possibilities. It offers a point of contact for the new homeschooler: a place to find out that their children are really not worse than everyone else's. It offers the veteran homeschooler a tangible way to encourage and minister to those in need of a kind word, a helping hand, or regular mention in prayer. It offers creative and energetic people an outlet for the blessings that their gifts generate, such as a play, Christmas decorations, extra activities or art classes. It gives the organizers a chance to do what they do well, bring order and consistency to good intentions. In short, Park Day gives us a chance to function as a group with the common bonds of faith and service.

Initially, Park Days are often held out to questioning friends and relatives as evidence of opportunities to socialize. (This is just as true for the moms and dads as it is for the children!) As you continue on as a homeschooler, Park Days become opportunities to build needed friendships. Homeschoolers who feel isolated and alone can be worn down by the pressures of family, public schools or neighbors. A Park Day gives time for sharing struggles and concerns, as well as successes. Support groups and Park Days provide needed points of reference for feelings that are common to homeschoolers.

Children also build relationships during these times of fellowship. New homeschoolers who have been recently removed from a public or private school setting particularly need to see other kids like themselves who are also homeschoolers. With new families, children can be welcomed into the group as parents are meeting one another and child supervision is still maintained. Under the watchful eye of parents, problems and conflicts can and should be addressed with a firm but merciful approach.

As a veteran observer, I can say that adult supervision of children is a touchy aspect of Park Day. Many parents become very defensive if someone tells on their child, or if their child is corrected by another adult. While the reasons for this are many and varied, the response to it should be consistent: the love that covers the sins of another. Scripture admonishes us to *speak the truth in love* to one another.

If Johnny hauled off and hit your little Suzie, try to find out what happened before upbraiding Johnny and his mother. The most insidious problem that can crop up in homeschooling circles is the parent who cannot or will not see the truth about his or her own children's behavior. Whether one is a prominent leader or new homeschooler, we all share the same condition. We are all fallen, in need of God's mercy and grace, and capable of missing the mark. This should encourage all of us. Every child, not just yours, will misbehave at some time or other. Every parent will struggle with something, not just you. If we can pursue an open and teachable attitude, we may help our children avoid the painful results of the spiritual blindness caused by pride.

Scripture also encourages us to remove the beam

out of our own eye before we try to take the speck out of our brother's eye. Looking at other people's children critically does not amount to truthfulness. If Sally's children seem out of control, and Sally is doing her best to deal with them, then you have several options. You can try to help Sally by holding the baby or getting the lunches out. By so doing, you free Sally to do the disciplining. You can pray for Sally. If you haven't put in any time praying for Sally in her struggles, then please don't offer criticisms in the form of suggestions.

Outside of those two options, there is not much that will bear good fruit. If a particular child or family really causes problems, prayerfully seek the advice of your spouse, the group leader, or a mature veteran homeschooler. Much can be made of our differences in a group like this, and Satan's goal is always to divide. It takes an active effort to pursue the peace of God in these circumstances, and it takes humility to seek others' well-being.

Another important aspect of Park Day is hospitality. New homeschoolers have many issues to deal with and may arrive at Park Day like a desert traveler thirsty for water. Those who have been in the group for even six months have a great deal to offer these newcomers in the way of encouragement, acceptance and reassurance. Park Days can unfortunately become very cliquish, excluding those in true need of fellowship. Take the time to go beyond your regular circle of friends. Talk to new members or visitors. Invite them to sit with you at lunchtime. You probably see your old friends at other times as well, so ask God to use you as an ambassador of His love to new homeschoolers. The cup of cool water you offer them may be invaluable.

The last aspect of Park Day I will address is one of the most important: service. After attending several conferences for leaders, and visiting and listening to leaders across the country, I have learned that one of the most difficult problems they face is burn-out. Once someone takes on a leadership responsibility it seems that everyone else in the group assumes they will fill that slot for the rest of their lives. It may be difficult to get people to volunteer because they see others being crushed by the weight of the year-in and year-out responsibility. Leaders need to be able and willing to relinquish their responsibilities, as the Lord leads, and others need to be praying about how they can best serve the group. If the group's leadership is always held by a few of the longtime veterans, emerging leadership is not encouraged, nor are people functioning in their gifts.

Leaders should pray for God to raise up people who can serve the group and eventually take their places. Individual control or the seeking of personal power is not the model of leadership set in Scripture. We must not allow our homeschooling support groups or associations to become vehicles that exalt a leader or a person. Rather, these groups must pay tribute to all of the members, and more importantly, the Lord who enables us to homeschool in the first place.

To do this, we must have members who are willing to serve. As we often find in the Bible, the rewards don't always go to the most visible or the most glamorous. They often go to the unseen worker, the faithful servant, the unassuming person.

I know a woman in our group who many years ago wondered about her ability to be a good wife and mother. Married before she was a Christian, and with an unsaved husband, she struggled with her worthiness to be used by the Lord. She began to homeschool, uncertain at first, yet trusting in God. With a limited income, and the need to work at night, she clung to the course she felt was laid before her. Now with four children and exhausting physical demands, I see her frequently at homeschool and church events. She inspires me every time I see her. She has blossomed as a wife, mother, homeschooler and Christian, who reflects a joy in the Lord that is not circumstantial. She reaches out to the newcomers often, and has become a wise counselor to younger mothers. She has accepted some responsibilities in our support group, feeling the Lord is asking her to serve. She has heard the call of the Lord in many areas, and has stepped up to be a vessel for His use. This lady has shown me repeatedly that all God needs is a willing, obedient heart.

May we all be available vessels for His use in our support groups and Park Day groups. May we all seek to serve Him with our gifts and talents, with our hospitality and compassion. May we demonstrate to our children, our friends and newcomers the love that makes the way for His power to be made known.

---- ❧ ----

The Law of Love

As homeschoolers, we are part of the homeschooling movement. As individual Christians, we are part of the Body of Christ. While we remain individuals in each case, free to fulfill our callings in ways that express the gifts and talents God has given us, we also remain parts of the larger whole of Christian community.

Achieving unity is difficult, as you can tell from almost any endeavor that combines individuals focusing on a common goal. In and of ourselves, unity seems impossible to gain because it appears to require perfect agreement. How can we solve the dilemma of obtaining unity while maintaining our uniqueness as God's creations? How can we demonstrate the kind of harmony to the world that gives people hope for their own family, church or even nation?

Romans 13:8 says, ***Owe nothing to anyone except to love one another; for he who loves his neighbour has fulfilled the law.*** I believe our hope for the kind of unity that can be a light in great darkness is through the law of love. Love gives when it is not required to give. It prefers others over itself. It forgives when it would seem more just to judge. Love covers a multitude of true mistakes.

I have witnessed attitudes and actions among homeschoolers, (even prominent ones) that left me wondering. Are we not bound to the same law of love as Christian homeschoolers that we are bound to as Christians? While homeschooling may have become a "market," or a "political force," or even a mix of loyal supporters of particular homeschooling styles or leaders, we have not been released from being parts of the Body of Christ. We certainly have not, therefore, been released from the law of love.

How should we behave as Christian homeschoolers? The same way we should behave as Christians. We should be open to and respect the input of our brothers and sisters, not allowing allegiance to individuals to bring division to the Body of Christ. (I Corinthians 1:11-13.) We should encourage one another's successes and believe the best of each other.

If we fail to walk in the requirements that God has given to His people, we can be sure that He will deal with us. He loves us enough to treat us as His children. Don't make excuses for attitudes and actions within your homeschooling life that you know are wrong-spirited. Examine yourself and be open to God's correction. Otherwise, we will become like the Pharisees, congratulating ourselves on our holiness and the fact that we are not like others. Just being different in our lifestyle is not enough, we have to be different in our hearts.

Encouragement for Dads

My heart's cry for homeschooling dads is that they each will homeschool in their own fashion. I long for them to have freedom, with no standard of homeschooling correctness imposed upon them, other than what Scripture directs fathers and parents to do. Encouragement and challenges are fine, but ultimately authors and speakers do not answer to God for other men's children. The dads themselves do. Dad must be free to lead his homeschooling family in such a way as to produce peace and fruit in the home.

In Scripture, men were often directed by God to do things that did not seem to conform to the religious order of the day. God used these men powerfully as they obeyed what God called them individually to do. This was often different than what their neighbors, family members or even brethren were doing.

Homeschooling mothers must show their children that they trust the leadership God has provided through their husbands. This may mean gratefully accepting husbands whose contributions to homeschooling are long, hard days at the office, playing with little ones after work or fishing trips on the weekend with older children.

Many men desire to be more involved, but are legitimately restrained by demanding schedules. Their wives must appreciate the time these men offer, rather than lamenting the fact that it is brief. They must encourage their husbands to lead the way, and then trust God to direct their paths.

If your husband does not participate directly in your homeschool, and is nevertheless sure that he is obeying God, don't come under condemnation. Your homeschooling is just as adequate as anyone's. Take the matter to prayer, asking the Lord to give you greater appreciation for your husband's style of leadership and the way God wants him to be involved. It may be active involvement, or it may be just his blessing. If you still feel the need, then discuss this openly with your husband.

If your husband desires to participate more, talk with him to find out what would work out best for everyone. If your recommendations are unworkable or burdensome, relax and let God direct. Trust your husband, and trust God concerning his role in homeschooling. This will be a wonderful example to your children of **Ephesians 5:33,** which says: ***and let the wife see to it that she respects her husband.***

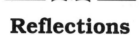

Reflections

How can you stand in the face of criticism from family and friends? (By remembering you are called to homeschool!)

Think about what motivates you as a homeschooler. Why do you do what you do? Are you worrying too much about pleasing people instead of pleasing the Lord?

Are there ways you can serve and minister to other homeschoolers? Pray about ways that you can share God's love with other homeschoolers.

Chapter Seven

Introduction: Evaluating Your Homeschool — Using the Right Measures

There are many things about your children and your homeschooling that you will want to evaluate from time to time. As with any other work in progress, it is good to step back from it occasionally to get a better view or a better perspective. How can we as homeschoolers do this in a beneficial way?

The first thing to remember is that there are many kinds of evaluation. You may want to consider annually or semi-annually the progress your child is making. Is he or she moving at the rate you expected? Do you know what rate you should expect? Be careful, because your child's progress should not be the only factor you consider. One day he or she could seem like a genius, and the next day not remember the most basic facts. This inconsistency is normal with children, so remember that your overall assessment is what counts.

Is your child able, with appropriate review, to give you the basic content you have covered in a particular area? If the answer is "Yes," you have evaluated one aspect of your child's abilities. You can be either encouraged or discouraged at different times by your child's progress, so don't make that your only criteria. I remember doing better in some grades than others, don't you? Try to look at this in the context of the overall picture.

Another popular tool of measurement is comparing your children's progress or abilities with generally accepted guidelines. As I have stated before, I believe one of the blessings of homeschooling is the freedom to be individuals. General comparisons with scope and sequences or age or grade level guidelines may help us plan more effectively. The danger, however, is that these comparisons can cause us to be overly demanding and stressed. I generally suggest that people take portions of these types of guides and follow them, but not to try to accomplish every item.

The decision to follow a certain guide or set of requirements should always be made in light of God's leading for the individual child or family. There are things I emphasized with my daughter in language arts that I did not emphasize with my son. He didn't seem to need that, and she did, or vice versa. Guides are good, but they must remain only guides, and not become taskmasters. Don't give up teaching a subject or topic that your children are motivated to learn about just because something else is in the guide.

Comparing your children to other children you actually know probably will not be fruitful or encouraging. Whether your children compare favorably or poorly, the process of comparison causes you to compete with the goals, gifts, talents or struggles that God has given another family. You will always be comparing apples to oranges. Fixing your gaze on someone else's path only pulls you off your own course. The discouragement you receive will most likely slow your progress.

At what age your child reads, how fast he or she matures, how your child does in math or creative writing, etc. are all things that have an individual time table. It is just the same as when a child learns to walk or talk. While a parent may take pride in an early walker, this does not make someone else's child better than yours. Reading earlier does not necessarily mean that Johnny is smarter than Suzie. It merely means Johnny was ready to read earlier (or was forced to read earlier). In the final analysis, the goal for both children is the same: to read and comprehend. Seek to know God's timetable for your child, and adjust your plans accordingly.

Many times parents have learned this truth the hard way, by placing standards on their children that were unreasonable. They may have ended up with crying, resistant children or children who just didn't want to learn anymore. While no child wants to learn everything, there is a natural desire in children which can be encouraged through reasonable teaching methods. If you look at a textbook or topic and think, "How boring," chances are your children may not fare much better. Please take interest into consideration. This step will reap great rewards.

Remember that all homeschoolers (both parents and children) have days when they don't want to homeschool. This is normal and nothing to be alarmed about. If those days are starting to outnumber the good days, find a veteran homeschooler or friend you can talk to. Don't assume the problem is you. Often, schedules can be adjusted or even materials changed, making a great difference in how everyone feels.

Most of all, remember that feelings are not what we base decisions about homeschooling on. We homeschool because we are called to, not because we always feel like it, or it is always fun. This is good news because it can take an emotional burden off of you. If things seem difficult for long periods of time you may want to get with your spouse and re-evaluate.

First-time homeschoolers, especially those whose children were previously in public or private school, need to know that things may seem trying for awhile. Many adjustments need to be made, so give yourself at least a year to get settled. After that, you can address trouble spots as they arise.

I have saved the most stressful aspect of evaluation for last. Standardized testing. Usually, the panicky feelings begin right after Christmas. Depending on the test results, they may stop in April or May. If the test results don't seem up to snuff, these feelings of fear and inadequacy can linger all summer. How do I know? I've observed many homeschoolers go through this process year after year. I've even had a twinge or two of uncertainty myself when my children take their tests.

Is this just the lot of homeschoolers, going through anxiety year after year? I don't believe it has to be. In the previous chapter, we established the best way to handle the ups and downs of family and friends' reactions to homeschooling. This is to remember that we homeschool because God has called us to do it. We believe that it is best for our children. Does that mean we shouldn't be diligent with our schoolwork or that we can be unconcerned about test results? Of course not, but we don't have to be controlled by the fear of failing.

When we begin to require our students to do certain types of busy work or to study harder to make us feel better, we are acting out of fear. While this may be a natural response in our flesh, this is not God's desire for us.

Test results are just one piece of information about your child. If you don't think they are accurate, get another opinion. Take the results and add them to the other measures you consider, such as overall progress. The homeschooling law in Florida states it this way: *"A child must make progress commensurate with his ability."* Comparing your child's results to his or her own previous results may be a good way to be assured that your child is doing fine. Making a year's progress from his or her last scores would usually be acceptable.

Don't allow yourself or your children to be robbed of the satisfaction you have earned during your homeschooling year. Put on your detective's hat, and go to work to find the evidence of progress and success. Become your child's advocate by not taking a bad test score as the whole truth about his or her ability. Find the real truth about your child's achievement and then use the test results as a planning tool, rather than a club with which to beat either your child or yourself.

──── ❧ ────

Taking Stock,
Not Measuring Up

Many of us homeschool without regard to the traditional school schedule. We take advantage of the wonderful field trip and science opportunities in summer. Still, our family needs to take a break. The long evenings of light in the summer beckon us to stay outside. We savor the time to read for pleasure, complete a put-off project, or just have fun with family and friends.

With summer vacation comes the inevitable looking back over the year, recalling triumphs, and reconsidering the tough times. During the summer you can take stock of where you and your children are in terms of homeschooling. This does not have to be an ordeal. Evaluating your children's progress does not have to be a time of trying to measure up!

As a certified teacher in Florida, I often evaluate homeschooled children in order to fulfill the annual state and local requirement. I take this opportunity to share with many anxious parents and tense children that test results are just one piece of information about a child. It may not be the most valid or revealing piece of information either.

When I spend two hours evaluating a child, I get to know a young person who has been given gifts and talents by God and whose school year has been a mix of successes and trials. They are eager to show me art projects, or new brothers or sisters, or to tell me about their baseball season. They understand that life is more than evaluation and that they are more than the sum of their test results.

Not many parents are as free, however. Homeschoolers are a very diligent and responsible group. (Some people would say that we are "over-achievers.") Many good character qualities come out of such devotion, but it does have a down side. People who are diligent and responsible often can't separate the value of achieving outward success from the value of whom they are in the Lord. The lines between diligence and compulsion can blur when we begin to make decisions and evaluations based solely on outcomes. Outcomes are important, but as any teacher will tell you, the process can be just as important, if not more important, than the product.

What do I think constitutes a successful year of homeschooling? There are several elements which will appear in varying degrees from year to year.

1. Academic progress.

Notice that I didn't say academic perfection. I recently encountered a mother lamenting her daughter's progress in math. The mother told me that her child was struggling with two-place multiplication. I remained empathetic until I learned that her daughter was in second grade! I tried to graciously express my horror over her being required to master such a thing at that age. Our standards must be reasonable. If the curriculum you use is generally thought of as above grade level, or accelerated, please take this into account when evaluation time comes. Think of the adult response to the pressure to excel year after year. Your child is less equipped to cope with that than you are.

2. Increased maturity.

This is revolutionary when it occurs. Trying to accommodate God's timetable, rather than your timetable, for maturity will relieve a great deal of frustration in your homeschool. Young children usually fall into two categories: perfectionists who feel that they should master everything on the first try, and those who have yet to demonstrate (in your presence) that they think education will have any bearing on their lives. This latter group, especially if they're boys, usually already have an action-packed career picked out, and know that academic pursuits would just get in the way of practicing the perfect baseball swing. Cooperating with the "progress, not perfection" model will free you to see the subtle changes taking place. You'll notice longer attention span, more problem solving skills, effectiveness of discipline to produce self-control, etc. These developing qualities can be a cause for joyous celebration and may make superior academic skills seem less consuming.

3. Realized potential.

When I see a child who decodes words many levels above chronological age, yet comes completely unhinged at the thought of composing a few sentences in his or her own words, I feel that a disservice is occurring. This child's curriculum might have stressed things that produce success on the test, but the imbalance reveals the need for process, not just product! There are no easy-to-use formats for skills that require time, trial and error, thinking and rethinking. Such procedures, however, are essential for the higher level thinking processes our children need in order to realize their God-given potential. I don't think the country can tolerate another generation that merely achieves the minimum required of them. Always instructing to closed-end situations (fill in the blanks, multiple choice) promotes this kind of thinking. Academic success is demonstrated by reaching new levels in comprehension, creative writing, problem solving, and bringing up weak areas. In college, points are often given for having the process right, even if the answer is incorrect. There is value in the attempt and the practice. The answer will come eventually.

4. Emotional and spiritual well-being.

Sometimes the very best a homeschooling parent can hope for is a year of recovery. If a child has been in a public or private school setting that has been stressful or damaging, then a good year of homeschooling would be one that yields a happier, more responsive child. Secure children can take risks and express their thoughts without fear of rejection or humiliation. If your child has had difficult experiences, then emotional and spiritual progress would be a prime indicator of a successful year.

At least to a degree, success is in the eye of the beholder. While we all agree that progress is needed during a year of homeschooling, the types and extent of achievement vary. When I was a Special Education teacher, I often worked with children who could not feed themselves or perform other basic tasks alone. Moving to a "regular" second grade class, I was overwhelmed by the children's abilities. Because my class was the "low" group of second graders, the other teachers thought I was crazy for being so impressed. According to them, my students didn't measure up. Nevertheless, the children in that class made amazing progress that year. Hopefully, they learned to do their best, to realize that everyone has talents, and to be content with their best efforts.

As Christians, we are encouraged to do our work *as unto the Lord*. This principle influences all our efforts in life. Often, however, we can not control the results of those efforts. That requires trust in God.

> **Whatever you do, do your work heartily, as for the Lord rather than for men; knowing that from the Lord you will receive the reward of the inheritance. It is the Lord Christ whom you serve.**
>
> **Colossians 3:23, 24**

God's View
into Our Lives

Long ago, the prophet Samuel was sent to Bethlehem to select a king over Israel. He was sent to the house of Jesse, the father of eight sons. As he looked at each of seven sons, he waited for the confirmation of the Lord, yet it did not come. There, a great truth was spoken: ***"...God sees not as man sees, for man looks at the outward appearance, but the Lord looks at the heart."***
(I Samuel 16:7.)
Eventually, David was brought in and anointed by Samuel. Scripture tells us that ***"...the Spirit of the Lord came mightily upon David from that day forward."*** **(I Samuel 16:13.)** Samuel's tendency to judge by looks was natural.

Often, all we have to go by, it seems, is outward appearance. Much of society judges by how things look. We are judged by how attractive, how successful or how much in keeping with the standards of the day we are. Yet we who know Him as our Savior have received a great gift, a God who does not judge by outward appearance, but who sees into the very depths of our heart.

As a certified teacher, I've evaluated many children who come with worried, apologetic parents. The parents recount difficulties or unfinished assignments, usually taking the blame upon themselves. I encourage them to relax, to have faith in their children, and to trust the Lord. Without fail, the Lord meets us. The test results are usually fine, or, if there is a problem, a path becomes evident to lead to changes and improvements in the troubled area. God is faithful to these homeschoolers, not due to their outward appearance (of success or failure) but because of His relationship to those hearts, His commitment to be faithful to those He calls, and His love for all of His people.

When we think of God seeing into our hearts, it usually conjures up a sense of apprehension in us. "Oh, no," we say, "He can see all my sins, all my bad attitudes, all my failings." Well, that is true, but that is not all He sees. He also sees your commitment, your concern, your love and your efforts. He knows what you hoped for and desired, and He knows what you meant.

Should this matter to us? Isn't it only what gets done that counts? Isn't God's yardstick of measurement the same as mine? Thankfully, no. Scripture reminds us that our ways are not His ways (Isaiah 55:8), because His thoughts are higher than ours. Based only on the outward view, Jesus never would have forgiven the woman caught in adultery, or spoken to the Samaritan woman at the well. He wouldn't have associated with sinners and tax-collectors, and he probably would not have forgiven a convicted criminal from the cross.

Instead of looking only at the outward, as the Pharisees did, Jesus looked at the heart. The Pharisees were very secure in their good works and fine appearance. They were hard to find fault with outwardly but Jesus saw their motives. He said to them: ***"Now you Pharisees clean the outside of the cup and the platter; but inside of you, you are full of robbery and wickedness. You foolish ones, did not He who made the outside make the inside also?"*** **(Luke 11:39-40.)**

When you are hard on yourself because of what you have NOT accomplished, don't assume that the Lord is being hard on you, too. God is more than able to convict us of true sin, so we can rest in the knowledge that His view of our hearts will be accurate. When you feel inadequate, confused or uncertain about what to do, don't assume that the Lord sees you that way. He promises that His grace will be sufficient for all that you need, whether you recognize it or not. When you feel like a failure because your children don't perform like someone else's children, don't assume that you have failed. Examine the measuring stick carefully to make sure it is not one of your own making rather than one that the Lord has provided.

As testing time rolls around for your children, take heart. It is not testing you as a homeschooler, parent, or Christian. It is an indication of how much academic information your children have retained. As for the test of outward appearance, I encourage you to skip that one this year. Instead, set up an examination time with the Father. Lay your heart and your actions before Him. Share your triumphs and disappointments. Let Him see your doubts and fears, as well as your joy. Then give this year of homeschooling to Him as the sacrifice of one who sought to obey Him. You will be amazed and blessed by the results of your time with the Father who knows your heart.

> *Since therefore, brethren, we have confidence to enter the holy place by the blood of Jesus, by a new and living way which He inaugurated for us through the veil, that is, His flesh, and since we have a great priest over the house of God, let us draw near with a sincere heart in full assurance of faith, having our hearts sprinkled clean from an evil conscience and our bodies washed with pure water. Let us hold fast the confession of our hope without wavering, for He who promised is faithful.*
> **Hebrews 10:19-23**

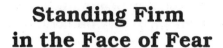

Standing Firm
in the Face of Fear

Starting back to school in January can be trying. Not only is it hard to get back into the routine, it is equally difficult to rekindle the sparks of motivation which were so prevalent in the fall. In most places the weather isn't much help either. Rain, cold or gray skies add to the sense of dreariness. While all these factors are hard to deal with, they really don't compare to the most difficult aspect of January: uncertainty about whether or not your children are learning all they need to know. In January it seems that testing time is just around the corner. The academic progress made before Christmas is a distant memory. These combined pressures lead to a state I call a homeschooling panic attack.

The first thing you need to know is that this panic is very common among homeschoolers. While it reveals a bit of our insecurity and self-doubt, it does not have to take control. Many people have come to me at conventions telling how they succumbed to this sense of panic, switched curriculum and approaches, and later regretted it. While I may believe that a certain approach to teaching and learning is superior, my main message is that our method is secondary. The true battle is in the area of our faith.

Review the plans you made in the fall. Remind yourself of the leading the Lord provided for you. Resist the temptation to compare yourself and your children to other homeschoolers. While it may seem difficult, stay on course. The counsel of the Lord which seemed so wise before has not changed. The peace your decisions brought in the fall is obtainable again. The condition is that you stand firm.

If you have wavered, don't feel bad, just make a decision to hang in there. If you have to make this decision more than once in the coming months, don't worry about it. The goal of our adversary is to get us off track. If we manage to stay on course, the enemy has failed. Remember, fear does not come from God. When we are motivated by fear, we are really responding to the enemy's lead. The fruit of our relationship with God includes peace and patience. (See Galatians 5:22, 23.)

Stand firmly, staying the course set for you by the Lord, determined to see the fruit of faithfulness prepared for those who are able to persevere while homeschooling.

> ***Therefore, take up the full armor of God, that you may be able to resist in the evil day, and having done everything, to stand firm.***
>
> **Ephesians 6:13**

Reflections

Every so often, look over the goals you wrote after Chapter 5. Use these goals as part of your evaluation process.

Ask God to show you how He feels about your homeschooling. Don't be afraid to ask Him to encourage you. Be observant of God's blessings on your efforts.

Remember the steps to take when you feel fearful:

1. Review the plans/decisions you made in the fall.
2. Remind yourself of the leading the Lord provided for you.
3. Resist the temptation to compare yourself and your children to others.
4. Rest in the knowledge that the Lord is in control.

Chapter Eight

Introduction: Remembering Who We Are

While sitting at a red light during rush hour one day, my mind turned to the bigger questions of life. Not that dinner, school, baseball practice and laundry weren't enough to fill the limited amount of coherent thought available to me that day, but somewhere in my mind, a nagging question lurked. Since there was no time in my schedule for lofty questions, I tried to push it aside. However, the left turn line was long and the light short, so I found myself again opening the topic for consideration. You may laugh, or think it's frivolous, but the question that kept pushing its way forward was simple yet profound. It was, "Who am I?"

At my age, pondering such an issue may surprise you. I like to think of it as healthy reflection. God has seemed to ordain human beings to live life in seasons or cycles. Gratefully, I am not the same person I was twenty years ago. While some aspects functioned in a vastly superior manner (I'm thinking metabolism here), the lessons and experiences gained over the years have become dear tutors and teachers. I feel fortunate not to be in the same place spiritually or emotionally as I was even ten years ago. It is fair to say that in many ways I am not the same person I was then.

If I'm not the same person I was, then maybe it is good to ask "Who am I?" Maybe we should all ask ourselves this question from time to time.

As usual, our answers begin with the practical. As a Christian homeschooler, I wear many hats. I am a wife and parent. I am a sister, friend, relative, neighbor and church member. I am someone's child and someone's mother. I am part of a family structure that needs me and depends upon me. I am part of a community of believers, bound together by love and fellowship. I am part of a group of homeschoolers who have taken on a great responsibility for their children's education and development. I am a citizen of a state and country where there are many freedoms and responsibilities to be maintained.

While this list sounds exhaustive (and exhausting!) there is a part of my heart that tells me to look deeper, to pause a minute to let a fuller answer settle on me. I remember asking myself this question as a twenty year old college student. Living with a Christian family, I had the needed time for school, work and fellowship. Being interested in marriage, I had been praying for the Lord's guidance. The place I was led to in Scripture was an interesting one. Psalm 45, verses 10-17, seemed to leap off the pages at me. The Lord was speaking to the deepest part of me, calling me His daughter. Not only His daughter, but the daughter of a King!

In my search for the future, I had found out the answer to my past and present as well. While the revelation of being a part of God's family had come to me when I experienced salvation at age 12, this was a different experience. This carried with it a sense of closeness and tenderness, a sense of being special to my Father. The peace and security that resulted enabled me to walk through the season of young adulthood and into marriage with the assurance of God's direction and the comfort of His guidance.

As I ponder again who I am, I am reminded of that special time and place in my life given by a loving Father. Was that just for my younger years, or is it a message I need to hear in my life right now?

While much of what I do fulfills me in its own unique way, there is a need for rest and security for all of us in today's world. We have been invited to sit at the feet of a loving and tender Father, to drink in His pleasure in us, to place complete faith and trust in this most important Person in our lives; in short, to be loved and cared for simply because of our relationship, not for our abilities or efforts.

We all know the effect of a father's love (or lack of it) on a child. Without this crucial care, we can feel unloved and unworthy. While many of us have had fathers who loved us, all of us need the wholeness offered by a divine Father. If you have lost your father due to death, divorce or just emotional distance, you have an open-ended invitation to be cherished and treasured by the most perfect Father available. Seek God your Father in prayer. Ask Him to show you how to trust Him and rest in His arms, as a child does. Ask Him to fill the areas of need in your life that may have been untended by your earthly father. Then, prepare yourself for the glorious results.

Why is this so important? If we are secure in the fact that we are loved and cherished, then we can deal with many things. We can endure, we can have faith and we can labor without recognition. We can do much of what our hearts desire to do because we are free. We are not performing for acceptance, or recognition, or to gain value. We can simply serve, as an outflow of what is in our hearts. We can come along side our spouse and children in times of stress and trouble without fear, because of the strong love of our Father. There is always a Father's ear to listen, a shoulder to cry upon and an arm to lean on. There is always a sense of Fatherly concern about our well being and our needs that we merely taste of with our earthly dads.

There will be too, those times of Fatherly encouragement to move on in an area of our lives, to forgive and to release, to mature, for that is also a natural outgrowth of a father-child relationship. He may love us unconditionally, but He is not like some parents who cannot see us the way we really are. He knows us intimately, yet He does not reject us.

As a woman, I often think of Proverbs 31. This passage provides a perfect example of what a secure, loved and appreciated woman can do. She did not do those things to obtain the love of her husband and the blessing of her children. I believe she did those many things because of the love and support she had already received.

The Proverbs 31 woman should not stand as a goal or a gauge of spiritual achievement, but rather as a testimony of the possibilities of a woman's life when she is given time, opportunity, assistance and encouragement. To try to do all the things she did without this strong undergirding would require striving, and would be exhausting and discouraging. We must seek the love and support of our Father first, and then let this love motivate and energize us.

What will the results be of renewing this all-important relationship between Father and child? The jobs you do as spouse, parent, sibling, neighbor, etc., will never be the same because these roles no longer define you. When we ask ourselves now who we are, we can answer with confidence, that although we may <u>do</u> all of the things described, above all, we are a much loved child of the King.

Keeping Test Results in Perspective

At this time of year, talk among homeschoolers inevitably turns towards testing. Those whose children do well on standardized tests are usually comfortable with the process, while other homeschoolers may have the stressed-out look of a defendant on trial.

For their children, unsuccessful testing experiences or failures in the classroom have created a less than ideal testing situation. For some younger children, the unfamiliar group setting, the unfamiliar adult and the inability to ask questions can be very upsetting. Telling a seven-year-old you can't help him with something he doesn't understand is very hard for him to understand. Eager to please children may find testing frustrating because of the lack of adult feedback.

As an evaluator of students in the public schools and an evaluator of homeschooled students for the last six years, it is my observation that test results do not always present an accurate picture of student achievement. So many factors influence test performance (stamina, temperature of the room, test presentation, hunger, etc.) that it is fair to say that standardized testing will not always give you correct information. Testing is not a fool-proof science, especially when we are talking about one test administered annually.

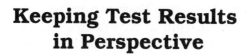

If your child does well, on standardized tests, you can use this form of evaluation comfortably. If your child's performance on standardized tests does not seem to be in keeping with his ability, seek a second opinion. See if your state or school allows teacher evaluations or portfolio evaluations, instead of only test results for your end of the year evaluation. Individually administered tests (such as the PIAT - Peabody Individual Achievement Test or the Kaufman Individual Achievement Test) also provide nationally normed scores yet are more in keeping with the homeschool setting. They can provide a great deal of useful information for teaching as well as test scores to turn in. Talk with homeschoolers in your area to determine what your options are, and try to remember, testing is only one piece of information about your child. It does not form a complete picture. If your child's test results seem inaccurate, pursue further assessment before you submit these scores to a county or school official.

Much of the stress related to testing for homeschoolers comes from the feeling that the test results are a final, unalterable judgment of you and your child. This doesn't have to be the case — know what your options are as you approach testing time, prepare prayerfully and then try to release yourself and your child from a do-or-die level of stress. Remember that God is in charge of our homeschooling, and as such, He is a trustworthy supervisor. As we offer Him our best efforts, as students and teachers, we can then rest, giving Him the burden of the test results.

——— ❧ ———

The Heart
of Homeschooling

As I sit down to write this column, I am nearing the end of curriculum fair season — that time of year marked by seeing old friends, meeting new people, giving and receiving encouragement, and lastly, being very, very tired. Please don't take this as complaining, it isn't. Like much of homeschooling life, it isn't bad, it's just the way it is. For several months, life seems to be at a whirlwind pace and there is much to be seen and done and ultimately, I am strengthened by the contacts with homeschoolers and the inspiration and encouragement they always generously give me. But at the end of even a good thing, I find myself longing for home and hearth, routine and life on an even keel.

You may ask yourself — what does this have to do with me? As we all begin a new school year, I think it's time to once again remind ourselves of what it is we are doing and why. You have chosen to accept the responsibility to educate your child. You will not be working with only his brain — his body and soul will be attached. You will see his heart and hear his dreams. You will see him at his best and his worst. You will probably have cabin fever, spring fever, great highs and lows and even boredom. You will see your children grow and mature and astonish you with their compassion, and then see the same little creatures fight and cry and whine over who-was-looking-at-whom. In short you will willingly board the cabin and strap yourself into the most intimidating, yet exciting, amusement park ride that exists — everyday life with your children. Before you run for the exit, let me point out the prize at the end of the ride.

During a curriculum fair here in Tampa, I was busily talking to people, preparing to give workshops and generally running around life a chicken. I had been in this state of high-level demand on my energy and faculties for several days, and was feeling rather dazed. I was waiting for a friend's workshop to begin, sitting off to the side of a large room. For the moment, I was alone. My eleven-year-old son, who had just arrived at the fair with my husband, came in the room looking for me. He saw me, came over and gave me a big hug and kiss on the cheek. He sat down next to me, put his arm around my shoulder and said, "How's it going, Mom?"

Since he knows me well, and never really wonders why I do these things anymore, I teared up and told him that I was doing much better now. He smiled and remained in that position in full view of at least 100 total strangers.

The eleven-year-old boy sitting next to me also has seen me at my best and worst, heard my dreams and seen my heart. He has seen me be kind, patient and crazed. He has asked me for forgiveness and he has forgiven me, many times. He has trusted me, yielded to my decisions, fought me on occasion and been a real helper to what I seem to become sometimes, the mother-over-the-edge. He sees the pressures and demands we face with the magazine, business, and ministry and he has prayed for us to be strong. He has chosen to patiently answer the frequent question, "How do you like homeschooling?" and he still is willing to be identified as my child after I have used him as an example of the baseball child who could have cared less about academics in my workshops.

He has, in essence, chosen to get into the cabin of the same intimidating, yet exciting amusement park ride and strap himself in with us. He has become an older child who is not perfect, but who has grown and flourished as a caring person who is secure being himself in our little homeschool. And although I am still one of the adults in charge, I can say that in him I see a man I will trust, and contrary to what the world offers in a family, I can say with grateful amazement, that he is my friend.

Remember as the days and weeks go by of this homeschooling year, that God is at work in us all, and He desires to craft families that reflect the strength of the rock that He gives us to stand on — ***We love, because He first loved us. (I John 4:19.)*** We need to see our children as friends that God is raising up in our midst — friends who know us and love us just the same. Friends who can lift our spirits and strengthen our hearts with a hug and a kiss. Friends for whom no sacrifice is too great.

Reflections

Remember your position as a daughter of the King. Think of the ways you relate to a father and apply those to your relationship with God the Father.

Try to put academic testing results into perspective. If your children are at an average level or above, be grateful and pray for ways to stimulate their love of learning and enjoyment of school. If your children do not score on an average level, pray for guidance concerning how to interpret the test information accurately, and to make any needed changes. Encourage love of learning and enjoyment of school in your children as well.

Don't forget to look at your children as friends in the making. Take steps to build a friendship with them, just like you would anyone else. This is especially important as they mature.